Pampering Your Pooch

Discover What Your Dog Needs, Wants, and Loves

Jason R. Rich

Howell Book House™

Howell Book House
Published by Wiley Publishing, Inc., Hoboken, New Jersey

For general information on our other products and services or to obtain technical support please contact our Customer Care Department within the U.S. at (800) 762-2974, outside the U.S. at (317) 572-3993 or fax (317) 572-4002.

Wiley also publishes its books in a variety of electronic formats. Some content that appears in print may not be available in electronic books. For more information about Wiley products, please visit our web site at www.wiley.com.

Library of Congress Cataloging-in-Publication data is available from the publisher upon request.

ISBN-13: 978-0-470-00922-2
ISBN-10: 0-470-00922-5

Printed in the United States of America
10   9   8   7   6   5   4   3   2   1

Book design by LeAndra Hosier
Illustrations by Sara McKinley
Cover design by Susan Olinsky
Book production by Wiley Publishing, Inc. Composition Services

Contents

Acknowledgments

Thanks to Pam Mourouzis at Howell Book House for making *Pampering Your Pooch* a reality, and for her continued support as we work on a variety of books together. Thanks also to Beth Adelman, my editor, for her hard work and dedication to this project. I'd also like to thank illustrator Sara McKinley, whose drawings you'll be seeing throughout the book.

My gratitude also goes out to all of the people at the various companies who supplied me with products to write about in this book and who provided much of the valuable information you'll soon be reading. Many of these people are truly dedicated to enriching the lives of dogs everywhere.

On a personal note, my love and gratitude goes out to my best friend, Mark Giordani, who has helped to train Rusty (my Yorkshire Terrier), as well as to Ferras AlQaisi (www.FerrasMusic.com), my dear friend who enriches my life in so many ways. My close circle of lifelong best friends wouldn't be complete, however, without acknowledging Ellen Bendremer, Sandy Bendremer, and their incredible children, Emily and Ryan.

I'd also like to acknowledge the love and support I continue to receive from my family, and congratulate my father on his recent marriage. Finally, I'd like to dedicate this book to my childhood dog, Snoopy; my coauthor on this project, Rusty (www.MyPalRusty.com); and to all of the pampered pooches out there who will benefit as their loving owners read this book.

As you spend your hard-earned money pampering your own dog, please remember all of the dogs who are less fortunate, including those who are homeless and who desperately need your help. Please consider supporting the amazing work done by the many reputable and hard-working animal charities and shelters throughout the country, through donations of your money and perhaps by volunteering your time.

Introduction

*D*ogs are our faithful companions. They provide unconditional love and affection, and are usually absolutely grateful for everything we do for them. They're sad when we leave home without them, but we can always count on a greeting filled with enthusiasm when we return. If you're one of the millions of people who adores their dog and considers him to be a member of the family, and you want to do absolutely everything within your power to keep your dog healthy and happy while at the same time providing him with the very best that life has to offer, you've picked up the right book!

If you follow the Hollywood scene, you already know that celebrities like Paris Hilton pamper their dogs with diamond-studded collars, designer outfits, and a wide range of other extravagant and fabulous items. This book will teach you how to expertly pamper your dog as well—but it won't be cheap!

This Is Not a Dog-Training Manual!

The very first thing you need to understand about *Pampering Your Pooch* is that this is *not* a dog-training manual! There are hundreds of books, videos, and training classes available if you want to train your dog. (In fact, I definitely recommend that in addition to pampering your dog, you begin training him as early in his life as possible.)

Rather, this book is all about expressing love for your dog by pampering him. You'll learn how to treat your dog to the best of everything life has to offer, while always keeping his health, well-being, and happiness in mind.

Just one way to pamper (not spoil) your dog is to make sure he's eating a well-balanced and healthy diet by offering him the very highest quality, best-tasting food available. It's *not* about spoiling your dog by giving him dozens of yummy supermarket-bought treats throughout the day—many of which are unhealthy or don't provide the well-balanced daily nutrition your dog needs. After all, you wouldn't feed a child an all-candy diet, would you? You need to strike a balance. And when you want to give your dog a treat as a reward, a show of affection, or a training tool, this book will help you choose from the most healthy and delicious treats and biscuits available.

It's okay to spend excessive amounts of money on your dog to provide him with the very best, as long as what you're giving him is beneficial. Spending hundreds or even thousands of dollars on a designer carrier, for example, so you can tote your dog around town in style is totally fine, as long as the carrier you choose is well made, the right size for your dog, and suitable for him. You never want to stuff your dog into a tiny carrier, simply because it's fashionable or the carrier you like happens to match your favorite outfit, purse, or the upholstery in your Mercedes.

You'll read about designer outfits for your dog, like this adorable baby blue and lime green cashmere sweater from Louisdog.

Pampering your dog is *not* about you! It's about putting your dog first, by addressing his needs. Only then should you consider matching up those needs with what you like and what's fashionable, trendy, or convenient for you.

Your dog is not a fashion accessory, like a purse, a wristwatch, or a scarf. He's a living creature who relies on you to care for him and love him. The health, well-being, and happiness of your dog are your first priorities. With that in mind, in this book you'll discover dozens of ways to dress him fashionably in designer outfits; use the most stylish and exotic collars, leashes, and identification tags; carry him in a designer-chic yet highly functional carrier; feed him the healthiest diet possible; occupy him with the very best toys available; and let him sleep or relax in the most extravagant and comfortable dog bed that your money can buy.

Plus, by reading *Pampering Your Pooch*, you'll discover the importance of having pet insurance and learn how to pamper your pooch by offering him regular massages, Reiki treatments, and proper grooming. You might even decide that an appointment with a pet psychic will help you better communicate with your dog. If you ever need to leave your dog while you're at work or traveling, this book also offers information about high-end doggy daycare and dog resorts. You'll also find detailed information about how to travel in comfort and style with your dog.

There are more than 68 million dogs in the United States. Every year, people spend more than $31 billion caring for their pets. It's therefore no surprise that high-end designers and companies such as Coach, Louis Vuitton, Gucci, Polo Ralph Lauren, Burberry, Marc Jacobs, Tiffany & Co., Nicole Miller, Harley Davidson, Orvis, Juicy Couture, Donald J. Pliner, and Life Is Good have begun offering premium-quality designer products specifically for dogs.

As you'll discover, there are also companies such as Posh Pooch, Twil Animal, The Pet's Jeweler, Roxy Hunt Couture, and Pets at Play that manufacture only high-end dog products and fashions that cost hundreds or even thousands of dollars. You'll only find these products at exclusive pet boutiques or online—they're not available at your local pet supply superstore.

With many of the high-fashion items, such as outfits and carriers for your pampered pooch, you'll learn that, like the fashion industry for people, styles change every season. By visiting the web sites of the various designers mentioned here, you'll be able to see the very latest fashion styles and trends.

Meet Rusty, the Yorkshire Terrier

Throughout this book you'll see Rusty, my pampered Yorkshire Terrier. Rusty was born on January 31, 2005, and has been my inspiration. As I was writing about many of the high-end products and services featured throughout *Pampering Your Pooch*, Rusty happily tested everything. He also served as a model in some of the photographs you'll soon be seeing.

You can learn more about Rusty by visiting his official web site at www.MyPalRusty.com. You can also visit my web site at www.JasonRich.com or email me at jr7777@aol.com. We look forward to receiving your feedback and hearing your innovative ideas on ways you pamper your own dog.

Author Jason R. Rich with his pampered pooch, Rusty.

1

Dog Food

Healthy Gourmet Fare for Your Discriminating Canine

here are countless ways to show your dog affection and pamper him with the very best of everything money can buy. Your favorite pooch might look adorable in a Gucci collar while being carried around in a Louis Vuitton carrier and wearing a cashmere sweater from Louisdog. But the very first step in truly pampering your dog is to focus on his health and nutrition. Providing a well-balanced and healthy diet could extend his life span and help avoid medical problems, which might require expensive and stressful visits to the vet.

Supermarkets and pet supply superstores carry a wide range of well-known dog food brands. But, have you ever actually read the labels to learn what's in those foods? All dog foods are definitely not created equal in terms of ingredients and nutritional value. Plus, the amount of money you spend on food doesn't always reflect the quality or nutritional value of what you're buying.

On your quest to find the best dog food for your pampered pooch, step one is to learn about your many options. In addition to the dog foods sold at your local supermarket and pet supply superstores, many of the best premium dog food brands are available exclusively through smaller, independent stores or online.

Innova, from Natura Pet Products, is one of many examples of a pet food brand that focuses on selling only healthy, nutritious, chemical-free, and natural ingredients. Plus, the manufacturing process follows the same strict standards that are applied to food for humans. According to Paul French, marketing director at Natura Pet Products, "Where the food is made is just as important as the ingredients put into it. Most pet food is manufactured in facilities that are not suitable for human food manufacturing, because the requirements and standards for pet foods are very different. For one thing, most pet food manufacturing facilities are not USDA inspected . . . in terms of quality assurance. Our manufacturing plants follow the same standards as a human food production plant."

Focus on Ingredients

Just because your dog eats the food you give him doesn't mean it's good for him. Look at the list of ingredients in the dog food as you would look at a menu. The ingredients are listed in descending order, by weight. But even if the first item listed is good, check out the next five or six items, taken together, because it's these items that mainly comprise what your dog will be eating. And if the very last item in the ingredients list is broccoli, for example, only a small amount has been added so the manufacturer can promote the fact that vegetables have been added.

If you don't know exactly what something is, think twice about feeding it to your dog. Also watch out for vague terms. "Meat and bone meal," for example, could mean it originated from anything red blooded. "Poultry fat" can come from anything with feathers. Find a brand that has all-natural ingredients, so you know what your dog is getting.

A premium brand of dog food will typically cost anywhere from 20 to 35 percent more than regular supermarket brands, but your dog will be healthier as a result, ultimately saving you a lot in veterinary bills throughout your pet's life. Also, in terms of volume consumed, you'll typically need to feed your dog less of a premium brand for him to get the same or better nutritional value.

A well-fed dog should not have itchy and dry skin, smelly ears, a runny nose, or watery eyes; these can be symptoms of a poor diet. When you switch from a low-quality dog food to a premium food, you'll see positive results in your dog, often within two weeks. For example, you'll notice his eyes will be clearer, his coat will be shinier, his breath will smell better, he may have more energy, and his overall health will be improved.

Canned or Kibbles?

Many veterinarians will tell you that for small dogs and puppies, kibbles (dry food) are better for their teeth. If you feed your dog hard biscuits as treats and brush his teeth, however, this has the same effect, so soft (canned) food is totally acceptable.

Tip For help choosing the ideal dog food for your pampered pooch, consult with your veterinarian and local pet supply shop, plus do your own research by visiting the web sites of the various pet food companies.

From a nutritional standpoint, if you compare the canned and dry versions of the same dog food brand, they're almost always identical. In most cases, the big difference is that canned food contains more water and dry food contains more grains. Many dogs will help you make the decision about dry or canned food, because they'll show a definite preference.

Choosing the Right Formula

Most dog food brands offer different formulas designed for the different life stages of a dog and sometimes for various breed groups or sizes. The best way to decide which formula is appropriate for your dog is to learn about his life expectancy. Dogs with longer life expectancies should remain on the puppy formula longer, for example, because it takes them longer to be fully grown. Your veterinarian will help you determine when your dog is considered a puppy, an adult dog, or a senior, and will also help you decide if your dog has specific dietary needs, based on a medical condition or allergies.

There are some dog food brands that offer one formula for all ages and breeds of dogs. In most cases, this food is just as nutritious and healthy for your dog as feeding him an age-appropriate or breed-appropriate formula. With the exception of puppy formulas, the idea of different formulas of dog foods was originally a marketing concept created by the major manufacturers to get more space on store shelves.

Tip If you decide to switch dog food brands or formulas, make the transition slowly and watch for allergic reactions. For up to ten days, mix a small amount of the new food in with your dog's current food. Each day, gradually add more of the new food until your dog is eating only the new food. You can make the change a little faster if you see no negative reactions.

Some older dogs may have health conditions that require them to eat a diet that's lower in salt or protein or fat; your veterinarian can tell you if that's the case with your dog. However, research has shown that puppies have unique dietary needs that are addressed in puppy-specific formulas, especially when you're dealing with premium dog foods. So while your dog is still a puppy, make sure he's eating food that's appropriate for his needs.

Dog Food Can Be Mixed with People Food . . . Occasionally

Dog food is specifically formulated to provide your pet with a well-balanced, nutritious diet. If you supplement this occasionally with a few leftovers or special treats, that's usually fine. To people, dog food doesn't usually look too appetizing, so we tend to want to jazz it up by supplementing it with the food we're eating. But too much of a good thing will throw off the "balanced" part of your dog's balanced diet. Limit the extras to no more than 10 percent of your dog's overall diet. Avoid overfeeding him and watch out for choking hazards, such as bones or wads of soft cheese.

Does Your Dog Need a Variety of Flavors?

Some dog food brands have chicken, beef, lamb, and even fish flavors and promote the fact that you can offer your dog variety in his diet. The fact is, as long as the food you're offering meets your dog's nutritional needs, there's no need for variety. This, too, is a marketing ploy. A dog does not wake up in the morning craving beef one day and chicken the next. Dogs are opportunistic eaters. They'll usually eat what they're fed.

If you're feeding your dog a very low-end brand of dog food, offering a variety can be good because you won't be exposing your dog to the same chemicals, additives, and preservatives day after day. But if you're feeding him a premium, all-natural brand, this is not an issue.

If you still want to pamper your dog with a variety of flavors, you can do this with treats and biscuits.

Dog Food Selection Checklist

Here are some things to consider when choosing your dog's food:

◆ Does the dog food offer a well-balanced diet, using all-natural ingredients?

◆ When reading the food's packaging, do you understand what all of the ingredients are?

◆ Is the manufacturer reputable?

◆ Are you feeding your dog the correct amount of food, based on his age, weight, and activity level?

◆ Are you keeping your dog's diet consistent? Try to avoid mixing or replacing dog food brands too often.

The Right Amount of Food

It's important to feed your dog the right amount of food each day so he can maintain a healthy weight. Your veterinarian, the food's packaging, and the manufacturer's web site will be able to offer you guidance about how much and how often to feed your dog. Puppies, for example, often require several small meals throughout the day, while older dogs can be fed once or twice per day. There are some dogs who will eat a few bites here and there throughout the day, but refuse to stick to a strict eating schedule. Whatever feeding schedule works for your dog, go with it.

To figure out how much to feed, start with the guidelines on the dog food's packaging. But keep in mind that the guidelines are based on averages and can vary based on the energy and the activity level of your dog. The quantity of food you should give your dog will vary, based on the brand of dog food, your dog's age, his weight, how active he is, and even how cold it is outside. Watch his weight, and adjust his portions accordingly.

One of the benefits of a premium dog food is that your dog usually needs to eat less of it because it's more nutrient dense. This means better health, less expense—and less cleaning up after the dog.

The Raw Diet Option

When it comes to feeding your favorite pooch, one of the most expensive options—but one that proponents say is the healthiest—is a raw food diet. The idea behind this type of diet is that for millions of years, wild dogs (and, in fact, all carnivorous animals) did not have owners who cooked their foods. It therefore stands to reason that dogs have evolved to be healthiest on a raw diet. By offering your dog raw (and absolutely fresh) beef, turkey, chicken, bones, whole eggs, fresh vegetables, fruits, and other healthy ingredients, you're providing your dog with the diet nature meant for him to have.

Raw diets are controversial, though, because not everyone believes raw meat is safe for dogs. Handling raw meat safely is also tricky. There are good arguments both for and against a raw diet, and it's definitely a good idea to do some more research before you decide to go raw.

What about cooking the meat? The problem here is that few people are willing or have the time to prepare complete, well-balanced meals for their dog every day. Dogs cannot live by meat alone, and if you prepare meals that lack some necessary ingredients, or those ingredients aren't fresh, your dog won't have a well-balanced diet, and he could ultimately become malnourished or ill. And if you buy a prepackaged, frozen raw diet, you're still relying on the manufacturer to make sure all the ingredients are appropriate and fresh.

A variety of dog food companies sell raw food diets. Each meal comes premixed, individually packaged, and frozen, with all of the ingredients for a well-rounded diet. To ensure your dog's health, however, the raw diet you offer must be well balanced and contain all of the nutrition he needs, which is why it's important to select the right raw food diet from a reputable company that offers a top-quality food.

Premium raw food diets can cost $5 or more per meal. To ensure maximum freshness, many of the companies that sell raw food diets tend to be small and only have regional distribution. However, many will ship the frozen meals directly to your home, weekly or every other week. Your veterinarian should be able to provide you with a referral. Before starting your dog on a raw food diet, or any new diet, consult with a veterinarian.

Premium Dog Foods

In addition to the many dog foods you'll find at your local supermarket and pet supply superstore, including Iams, Eukanuba, Pro Plan, and Hill's Science Diet, the following are just some of the premium dog foods currently available that can help keep your dog healthy and well fed.

Innova

Manufacturer: Natura Pet Products, Inc.
Phone: (800) 532-7261
Web site: www.naturapet.com
Availability: Online and from independent pet food and supply stores nationwide

If someone offered you fresh turkey, chicken, herring, apples, potatoes, carrots, whole eggs, and a variety of other fresh fruits and vegetables, you'd know you were eating right. Since 1990, these are just some of the all-natural ingredients that are in Innova's dog foods.

Innova uses fresh, whole ingredients from the five food groups, plus it adds probiotics and prebiotics for improved digestion and intestinal health. To maintain and improve your dog's skin and coat, omega-6 and omega-3 essential fatty acids are part of the food's formula, which is prepared using a three-stage cooking method developed to lock in natural flavors and nutrients.

By combining the right amount of human-grade, fresh, USDA-inspected meat, dairy, vegetables, fruits, and grains into every serving, Innova dog foods have superior quality and nutritional value with no added chemicals. Innova comes in a variety of dry and canned formulas, including Adult, Senior, Puppy, and Large Breed. To complement this healthy diet, Natura also makes Innova Healthbars as treats.

Some of the ingredients you *won't* find in Innova that are often found in other pet foods include meat meal, soybean meal, chicken by-products, poultry by-products, animal fat, poultry fat, rice flour, corn flour, wheat flour, rice bran, corn bran, peanut hulls, artificial flavors, artificial colors, BHA, BHT, and ethoxyquin.

For the organically inclined, Natura also makes Karma dry and canned foods, which are made from all-natural, 100-percent-certified organic products. According to the company, "Natura creates its Karma line from a holistic perspective, focusing on the quality of nutrition, balance and interaction of ingredients, and the addition of select nutraceuticals that improve and protect health. The philosophy of Karma Organic Food for dogs goes beyond the nutritional benefits with its philosophy of 'Good for the Body, Good for the Soul, Good for the Environment.'"

To learn more about the company's philosophy and products, visit its web site. The site also has a store locator.

Merrick Pet Food

Manufacturer: Merrick Pet Food
Phone: (800) 664-7387
Web site: www.merrickpetcare.com
Availability: Online and from independent pet food and supply stores nationwide

Established in the mid-1980s and based in Amarillo, Texas, Merrick Pet Care is a family-owned business that manufactures premium-quality dog food that's distributed exclusively through upscale pet supply stores. The company says it strives to produce the highest-quality pet foods and treats possible, using some of the best agricultural products available. The company boasts that it uses "human grade" ingredients, including fresh vegetables and fruits, plus USDA-inspected beef, buffalo, chicken, duck, lamb, trout, turkey, and venison. All of Merrick Pet Care's products are made in the United States.

Merrick Pet Food makes both dry and canned food, plus more than a hundred varieties of treats. The wide range of flavors have delicious-sounding names such as Wilderness Blend, Smothered Comfort, Venison Holiday Stew, Wingaling, Cowboy Cookout, Senior Medley, Turducken, Puppy Plate, and Grammy's Pot Pie. The company's Gourmet Variety 8-Pack offers a flavorful assortment. The canned food comes in two sizes, suitable for smaller or larger dogs.

All Dogs Need Water!

Just as important as the dog's food is the quality of his water. Your dog should always have access to fresh drinking water. Some people give their dog only filtered or bottled water, especially if their tap water contains chemicals or additives. Some upscale pet supply stores sell flavored water or vitamin water for dogs. Doggie Springs (973-692-9007; www.doggiesprings.com) is one company that makes a complete line of vitamin-enriched, flavored spring water for dogs.

Whether you decide to occasionally give your dog "enhanced" water products is up to you, but plenty of water is not optional. Replace the water in your dog's bowl at least two or three times a day to ensure freshness. Also, especially on hot days and after rigorous activity, make sure your dog stays hydrated.

Natural Choice

Manufacturer: Nutro Products, Inc.
Phone: (800) 833-5330
Web site: www.nutroproducts.com
Availability: Online and from independent pet food and supply stores nationwide

Since 1926, Nutro Products has been developing and manufacturing premium dog food. Like all premium dog food manufacturers, Nutro's emphasis is on using high-quality ingredients to create its three primary product lines: Nutro Max, Nutro Natural Choice, and Nutro Ultra. According to the company, "Natural Choice, for example, uses only the best ingredients that guarantee premium nutrition and superior performance. These benefits are visible in your dog's shiny coat, healthy skin, bright eyes, and overall look and feel of good health. . . . Our foods are naturally preserved with vitamin E. We never use chemicals like BHA, BHT, ethoxyquin, propyl gallate, or sodium hexametaphosphate."

The company's Ultra product line focuses on all-natural, holistic nutrition to promote a healthy immune system along with a well-balanced diet and overall good health.

Each of Nutro's product lines comes in dry or canned varieties, plus each product line includes an adult formula, weight control formula, large breed formula, and senior formula, plus several flavors. A store locator can be found on the company's web site.

Prairie

Manufacturer: Nature's Variety
Web site: www.naturesvariety.com
Availability: Online and from independent pet food and supply stores nationwide

Instead of offering separate formulas for dogs in various age groups, Nature's Variety has created a line of premium dry, canned, and raw foods suitable for all dogs. According to the company, "Nature's Variety believes many commercially available diets targeted at life stages or special needs (such as puppy, senior, large breed, weight control) are, in effect, formulation corrections designed to overcome nutritional deficiencies inherent in largely grain-based diets. These nutritional deficiencies arise from least-cost manufacturing practices that utilize large amounts of low-cost grain by-products, such as glutens. Glutens are generally included in kibble diets as a low-cost option to increase the protein content of the food without adding more meat. For this reason, Nature's Variety offers a nutritionally dense kibble formula that is appropriate for all life stages, based on high meat protein content and whole grains."

Unlike some other premium dog food companies, Nature's Variety's many formulas and flavors are designed to be rotated to provide your dog with optimal nutrition. For example, the company's dry kibble products come in Chicken and Rice Medley, Beef and Barley Medley, Lamb and Rice Medley, and New Zealand Venison Medley. The company reports, "The rotation regimen can play a role in building a healthier immune system, dental health, and addressing many common health concerns, such as food intolerance, obesity, allergies, digestive problems, and diabetes, some of which have been linked to continuous consumption of carbohydrate-based diets only."

As you'd expect from a premium dog food company, the manufacturing facilities owned and operated by Nature's Variety are built to USDA food standards for humans.

In addition to beef, fish, and chicken, some of the dozens of all-natural and healthy ingredients you'll find in Nature's Variety dog food include

Tip Store your dog's dry food in a sealed container at room temperature. Canned food can also be stored at room temperature until it's opened. Once opened, the unused portion of food should be refrigerated. Although dry dog food can sit out for a while, never leave uneaten canned food out for more than a few hours. Throw it out and replace it with fresh food, as needed.

alfalfa sprouts, apples, blueberries, broccoli, spinach, brown rice, carrots, flaxseed, honey, kelp, sweet potatoes, and wheat sprouts.

To help you formulate the right combination of foods and calculate the appropriate amount to feed your dog daily, be sure to visit the Nature's Variety web site, which offers interactive feeding guidelines. Click on the "Amount to Feed" icon.

Dick Van Patten's Natural Balance Pet Foods

Manufacturer: Natural Balance Pet Foods, Inc.
Phone: (800) 829-4493
Web site: www.naturalbalanceinc.com
Availability: From independent pet food and supply stores nationwide.

Actor and entrepreneur Dick Van Patten is a founder of Natural Balance Pet Foods, a company that creates extremely healthy diets for carnivores in zoos worldwide. More recently, Natural Balance Pet Foods developed foods for dogs and cats. On the company's web site, Van Patten explains, "My partners and I started Natural Balance Pet Foods more than sixteen years ago with the intention of developing the finest, healthiest pet food on the market. We wanted a pet food based on sound scientific principles and truth, not marketing hype. We did it! Not only for dogs and cats, but for large carnivores, such as lions, tigers, polar bears, and wolves in zoos and animal reserves worldwide. . . . Our Ultra Premium Formulas for dogs are scientifically formulated for all life stages, from puppies through adulthood. Our allergy formulas are made especially for puppies and dogs with specific allergies."

Celebrity Dog Food

Speaking of celebrities in the dog food business, Newman's Own Organics is a line of premium, organic dog food developed by the company owned by actor Paul Newman (now famous for his salad dressings and other gourmet foods for people). All the dog foods in the company's product line contain no genetically modified organisms and are produced without the use of herbicides or artificial fertilizers. Also, no chemical additives or preservatives are used. More than 70 percent of all ingredients used in the formulation of all Newman's Own Organic foods are organic.

The company offers both dry and canned dog food in adult and senior formulas. The dry foods are packaged in 5-, 12.5- and 25-pound bags, and the canned foods come in 12.7-ounce cans. Chicken and rice is the company's most popular flavor. A variety of healthy treats are also available. See the company's web site (www.newmansownorganics.com) for more information or to find a store near you.

Included in the company's dog food product line are Ultra Premium Dry Dog Foods, Ultra Premium Canned Formulas, Reduced Calorie Dry Formula, and Organic Formulas. They also make several flavor blends, such as Potato and Duck Dry Formula, Sweet Potato and Fish Dry Formula, Vegetarian Dry Formula, and Venison and Brown Rice Dry Formula.

Natural Balance Pet Foods offers top-quality canned foods, as well, in four flavors. Eatables canned food is designed to be eaten on its own or with the dry foods. It comes in adult and puppy varieties.

2

Treats and Biscuits

Pamper Your Dog with Healthy "Cookies"

Kids love candy, cookies, and anything that's sweet. But as a parent, it's your job to monitor what your kids enjoy to make sure they don't consume too much sugar and other unhealthy foods. Well, the same principle applies when you're raising and parenting your dog.

If you feed your dog a commercial dog food, whether it's Innova, Iams, Purina, or one of the dozens of other kibble or canned foods on the market, many of them, especially the premium brands, are specifically formulated to provide a well-balanced and healthy diet. While it's perfectly okay to reward your dog with a treat or a biscuit (something they love), you don't want to excessively feed her these goodies—they will ruin your dog's appetite for the healthy stuff, causing her to miss out on important nutrients, and can also disrupt a nutritious diet. Keep this in mind when giving your dog treats and biscuits.

When training your dog, a reward of yummy treats and/or biscuits is always welcome. It's also a great way to show your affection and periodically pamper your dog throughout the day, as long as you don't overdo it. For most dogs, a tummy rub, a walk outside, or a few minutes playing their favorite game is also a great reward. It doesn't always have to be food.

This chapter focuses on three types of treats: fruits and vegetables, homemade biscuits, and store-bought treats and biscuits. A *treat* is a small, usually soft, delicious snack for your dog, while a *biscuit* is a hard, cookielike snack. Many homemade and store-bought treats and biscuits come in a variety of flavors. While all are formulated for your dog to enjoy, you may notice she prefers certain flavors over others. To your dog, chicken, liver, bacon, cheese, and peanut butter flavors are like chocolate, strawberry, popcorn, caramel, and cotton candy for your kids.

Fruits and Vegetables Are Always Healthy Choices

Some raw fruits and vegetables make healthy treats that your dog will love. Some dog owners prefer to feed their dog organic or home-grown fruits and vegetables, but that's up you, based on how concerned you are about pesticides and other chemicals that are in supermarket-bought foods.

In his book *The Dog Whisperer* (Adams Media), author Paul Owens says one of the nine ingredients for the optimum health and growth of your dog is a high-quality diet. As part of your dog's diet, and as healthy rewards, Owens recommends, "Experiment to find the vegetables your dog likes best. Try grated raw zucchini, yellow squash, or carrots; chopped alfalfa sprouts; lightly steamed broccoli, asparagus, corn, green beans, turnips, parsnips, or peas. Try other vegetables to see how your dog responds, but avoid onions and cabbage because they can cause digestive upsets. . . . By adding some raw foods or high-quality supplements, you will be upgrading the quality and adding energy and nutrients to the diet." Owens says it's also okay to give your dog a small amount of raw fresh fruit, such as apples, grapes, and watermelon, several times a week.

> *Tip* Even when it's not part of a formal training session, whenever you give your dog a special treat, make her do a little work for it. For example, review her basic "sit," "down," and "stay" commands, then offer a treat as a reward for a job well done.

Dogs Love Boiled Chicken Breasts

If you go to any supermarket or pet supply store, you'll see dozens of chicken-flavored treats and biscuits. Well, if you want to give your dog a chicken treat that's totally free of additives, preservatives, and other chemicals, one easy way is to buy some organic chicken breasts at your local supermarket, boil them in a pot of water, cut the chicken up into tiny pieces, place those pieces in a resealable plastic bag or Tupperware container, and freeze them until you're ready to serve them to your dog. She will love them!

You can make a large batch that will last for a week or more, as long as you keep the unused snacks in the freezer. Because the chicken pieces are tiny, they thaw very quickly, and your dog will probably like them cold. Preparing this type of treat takes less than thirty minutes.

Your Love Is the Secret Ingredient in Homemade Biscuits

If you feed your dog canned food, many veterinarians recommend also giving her hard biscuits to help maintain her dental hygiene. Some dog owners prefer to cook those biscuits themselves, so they're totally free of chemicals, preservatives, and other unhealthy ingredients. Plus, when your dog sees you slaving in the kitchen, she'll know how loved she really is. Somehow, dogs know when that special ingredient, love, is added to their food. It makes everything taste that much better. And by baking your own dog biscuits, you know exactly what's in them and can fine-tune the recipe to include ingredients your dog loves.

Tip No matter what you feed your dog, it's important to periodically get her teeth professionally cleaned.

Baking your own dog biscuits is fun, very easy, and rewarding for both you and your dog. And you don't have to be a great chef to bake homemade biscuits your dog will love. You'll need only a few basic kitchen tools, such as a cookie sheet, oven, mixing bowl, rolling pin, measuring cup, spoons, and at least one cookie cutter, plus the ingredients, which can be purchased at any supermarket. The whole thing, from start to biscuit, takes less than thirty to forty-five minutes and is really easy.

You can find easy-to-follow dog biscuit recipes on the Internet. The following web sites offer a selection of free recipes you can print out. To find additional recipes, use any Internet search engine and enter the search phrase "free dog biscuit recipes."

✦ Gourmet Sleuth: www.gourmetsleuth.com/recipe_dogbiscuit.htm

✦ Rodney's Home Page: www.geocities.com/NapaValley/2049/doggie.htm

✦ Dog Biscuit Recipes: www.mce.k12tn.net/dogs/recipes/dog_biscuit_recipes.htm

✦ Good Dog Express: www.gooddogexpress.com/recipes.htm

✦ CutePuppyDog.com: www.cutepuppydog.com/Free_dog_biscuits_recipes.html

---

Cookbook for Dog Lovers

The Ultimate Dog Treat Cookbook by Liz Palika (Howell Book House, $14.99) is a 120-page, wonderfully written, easy-to-understand cookbook designed for dog lovers who don't necessarily know how to cook. The book is chock-full of yummy recipes that make baking dog treats and biscuits extremely simple. You'll also learn why certain ingredients are healthy for your dog, and discover fun ways to pamper your dog with these homemade goodies.

Buddy Biscuit Mix

Manufacturer: Cloud Star/Good Dog Express
Phone: (877) 682-PETS
Web site: www.gooddogexpress.com
Availability: Online

If you want to make homemade dog biscuits but don't want to stock up on all the ingredients from the supermarket, you can order Buddy Biscuit Bake at Home Treat Mix online. Each bag contains premixed ingredients for baking one of four flavors of biscuits: Apples 'n Oats, Cheese Delight, Chicken, or Molasses Madness. Each package will make approximately forty-eight biscuits, and a free dog-bone-shaped cookie cutter is included.

Making biscuits from a mix is just like baking from scratch.

When you're ready to bake the biscuits, you'll simply need to add oil and water. According to the manufacturer's web site, "All of our ingredients are FDA-approved for human consumption. No salt, sugar, preservatives, artificial colors, artificial flavors, or byproducts are added. Ingredients include unbleached white flour, whole wheat flour, dehydrated cooked chicken, lecithin, and a custom blend of natural herbs and spices."

Canine Cookie Cutters

Whether you use prepackaged dog biscuit mix or buy fresh ingredients at your local supermarket, chances are you'll want to make biscuits in fun, dog-themed shapes. Obviously, your dog won't care about the shape of the biscuit, but you don't want them confused with homemade cookies. Plus, the dog shapes add some levity to the baking process.

Tip Once your biscuits are cooked, let them cool before serving. Store the remaining biscuits in an airtight container, such as a resealable plastic bag or Tupperware. Keep in mind that, unlike store-bought biscuits, which contain preservatives, your homemade biscuits will only stay fresh for a few days.

The size of each biscuit will depend on the size and shape of the cookie cutter(s) you use. When deciding how large to make your biscuits, keep your dog's size in mind. Small dogs will prefer bite-size biscuits.

The following companies offer an assortment of dog-themed cookie cutters, in shapes that include dog bones, fire hydrants, dog paws, hearts, and even specific breeds of dogs. The cookie cutters are made of copper or tin and are available in several sizes. Prices range from $1 to $10 each.

✦ Birthday Express: www.birthdayexpress.com/bexpress/product.asp?sku=7876

✦ Copper Gifts: www.coppergifts.com

✦ Dog Like Nature: www.doglikenature.com/store/viewitem?item=80034

✦ Good Dog Express: www.gooddogexpress.com

✦ Pinocchio Productions: www.pinenose.com/ancocu.html

✦ The Victor Trading Company: www.victortradingco.com/dog.htm

Store-Bought Gourmet Treats and Biscuits

If you visit any supermarket, pet supply superstore, or local pet supply shop, you'll be able to choose from dozens of different types of dog treats and biscuits. They come in all shapes, colors, flavors, and sizes. Many, however, are loaded with sugar, artificial ingredients, preservatives, and chemicals—things your dog may think taste yummy but are not necessarily good for her to eat, especially in large quantities.

There are, however, plenty of healthy and even nutritious dog treats and biscuits on the market that your dog will love. Some are even designed to promote healthy dental hygiene. The following are just some of the more healthy treats and biscuits available.

Tip For more recommendations of healthy and nutritious treats for your dog, ask your veterinarian, especially if your dog is overweight, suffers from food allergies, or has any other medical condition.

Some store-bought treats that are available at supermarkets and pet supply superstores have flashy packaging and may be supported by multimillion-dollar advertising campaigns that claim how delicious these treats are, but your primary concern as a dog owner should be what's actually in the treats you'll be feeding your dog.

One extremely popular brand of dog treats, available at supermarkets and pet supply superstores nationwide, lists corn syrup, cornstarch, sugar, salt, propylene glycol, animal digest, bone phosphate, potassium chloride, phosphoric acid, sorbic acid, titanium dioxide, yellow 5, yellow 6, red 40, BHA, citric acid, and blue 1 among its ingredients. The front of the package proudly exclaims, however, "Made with real meat." Read the list of ingredients carefully and beware of ingredients you don't understand.

Greenies

Price: Varies, based on product size and quantity
Manufacturer: S&M NuTec, LLC
Phone: (816) 221-8538
Web site: www.greenies.com
Availability: Pet supply stores nationwide

Greenies are chew treats for dogs that are formulated to control dental tartar, plaque, gingivitis, and bad breath. These treats were the first to receive the Veterinary Oral Health Council's Seal of Acceptance to help control plaque and tartar. The manufacturer boasts that they're also formulated to taste great.

Greenies are shaped like a toothbrush and come in five sizes for various size dogs. Follow the manufacturer's guidelines when choosing which size is appropriate for your pampered pooch. Also, like all treats, this one is not designed to replace your dog's normal, well-balanced diet. Refrain from overfeeding your dog Greenies (or any other type of treat). In addition to her regular diet, the manufacturer recommends serving your dog one Greenie, not more than one or two times per day.

Nylabone Healthy Edibles

Price: Varies, based on product
Manufacturer: Nylabone Products
Phone: (800) 631-2188
Web site: www.nylabone.com
Availability: Pet supply stores nationwide

In addition to its immensely popular, nonedible Nylabone chew toys (see chapter 6), the company also has a line of Healthy Edible treats. Designed to compete with Greenies, Nylabone's Nutri Dent Brush Bones have what the manufacturer calls two breakthrough innovations: a "revolutionary 360-degree Power Action shape," which helps clean teeth and freshen breath; plus each bone is enriched with twenty-five vitamins, minerals, and omega fatty acids. Nutri Dent bones come in several sizes.

The company's other Healthy Edibles bones come in a variety of flavors, including cheese, BBQ chicken, peanut, lamb and rice, bacon, carrot, pork chop, and ham and cheese. They are available as singles or in combo packages. These chew treats make an excellent alternative to rawhide bones.

Innova HealthBars

Price: Varies, based on product size and quantity
Manufacturer: Natura Pet Products, Inc.
Phone: (800) 532-7261
Web site: www.naturapet.com
Availability: Pet supply stores nationwide

Innova HealthBars provide a tasty snack for your pampered pooch, but are also designed to be a nutrient-packed daily supplement. Just like Innova dog foods (see chapter 1), Natura Pet Products' recipes for its HealthBars use only fresh, whole ingredients from the five food groups: meat, dairy, fruit, grain, and vegetables. The biscuits are oven baked at low temperatures to preserve the valuable nutrients of the fresh ingredients and to maintain flavor and uniformity. HealthBars are available in small or large biscuit sizes, and in 26-ounce, 4-pound, and 20-pound packages.

Zuke's Mini Naturals

Price: $4.20 for a 6-ounce bag
Manufacturer: Zuke's
Phone: (866) 985-3364
Web site: www.zukes.com
Availability: Online and from pet supply stores nationwide

Great for dogs of all sizes, especially smaller ones, Zuke's Mini Naturals are soft treats that are perfect rewards during training sessions. The treats have the healthy benefits of rice, malted barley, and essential vitamins and minerals. They come in a variety of flavors that dogs usually love: salmon, peanut butter, and chicken.

The treats are tiny, fingernail-size pieces that are packaged in resealable plastic bags. For larger dogs, Zuke's also makes a variety of other tasty goodies, including bones, healthy jerky snacks, and Hip Action soft treats. The Hip Action treats contain 300 mg of glucosamine and 250 mg of chondroitin, plus essential cofactor vitamins, minerals, and amino acids, to promote hip joint flexibility and health.

Moo! Free Range Bully Sticks

Price: Varies, based on product size and quantity
Manufacturer: Free Range Dog Chews, Inc.
Phone: (586) 323-8004
Web site: www.freerangedogchews.com
Availability: Online and from select pet food stores nationwide

These tiny treats are great for training sessions with small dogs.

Many veterinarians caution against giving your dog rawhide bones, in part because some contain harmful chemicals. The problem is that rawhide comes from cattle, and the cattle come from various

Free-range cows in Brazil contribute to Moo! Dog Chews.

places throughout the world; some of these cattle are raised in less-than-desirable conditions. What sets the rawhide products from Free Range Dog Chews apart is that their Bully Sticks come from free-range Brazilian cattle that graze on the lush, green fields of Brazil and drink from fresh, clean springs and streams. These cattle are given no hormones or antibiotics, and no animal by-products are added to their diet. Brazilian cattle are therefore known as "green cattle."

All of Free Range Dog Chews' dog chews and bone products are manufactured in its own facilities in Brazil and are inspected at all stages of the manufacturing process. This process meets all USDA standards. The company's Bully Sticks and bones are odor-free and come in a wide range of sizes.

One caveat: Rawhide can also pose a choking hazard, which is why you should never leave your dog unattended with a rawhide chew of any type. Before giving your dog any rawhide product, consult with your veterinarian.

Halo Liv-A-Littles

Price: $9.98 for a 2.5-ounce package
Manufacturer: Halo Purely for Pets
Phone: (800) 426-4256
Web site: www.halopets.com
Availability: Online, and from natural food supermarkets and upscale pet boutiques nationwide

Halo Purely for Pets makes a wide range of natural and holistic foods and treats, including the Liv-A-Little line, which comes in chicken, salmon, beef, and cod varieties, all of which use only USDA-approved meats (suitable for human consumption). They are freeze-dried and come ready to eat. These treats are an excellent source of protein for your dog. From the company's web site, you can request a free copy of the company's holistic pet care booklet.

Dog Town Bites Premium Dog Biscuits

Price: $7 to $30 per package
Manufacturer: Dog Town Bites
Phone: (877) GO-FETCH
Web site: www.dogtownbites.com
Availability: Online and from carts in New York City

Dog Town Bites sells ultrapremium, freshly baked dog biscuits in more than a dozen varieties. These treats and biscuits—which resemble the kind of gourmet treats for people that you'd find at a Godiva store—use carob (not chocolate), nuts, and other organic ingredients to tickle your dog's taste buds.

You can order these gourmet treats and biscuits online, but the company also has several vendor carts that set up shop on the sidewalks of New York City on Fridays, Saturdays, and Sundays.

Fortunate Dog Cookies

Price: $11.95 for a box of seven cookies
Manufacturer: Rocky Mountain Labs, Inc.
Phone: (208) 726-6699
Web site: www.fortunatedogcookies.com
Availability: Online

Falling into the category of a cute gimmick, Fortunate Dog Cookies resemble Chinese fortune cookies, except they're designed for dogs. You'll have to help your dog read the printed fortunes within the cookies. There are more than 150 different messages, such as, "If what you want lies buried, DIG until you find it (but not in your neighbor's yard)."

Treat Pouch

During a training session (when treats or biscuits will be used as a reward) or while on a walk, you can keep your hands free by storing treats or biscuits in a handy, easy-access pouch that clips onto your belt. Available at pet supply stores, these small nylon bags come in many sizes and colors and are great for bringing treats with you when on the go. Doggone Good (www.doggonegood.com) is just one company that makes this type of pouch. They cost less than $10.

Packaged in a Chinese food take-out container, Fortunate Dog Cookies make a fun gift for dogs (and their owners). Each cookie is individually wrapped and is a liver-flavored treat for the dog. The cookies are made from basic ingredients, including liver powder, flour, sugar, margarine, and water.

Crunch Cards

Price: $3.95 to $5 each
Manufacturer: Crunchkins
Phone: (760) 328-1799
Web site: www.crunchkins.com
Availability: Upscale pet supply boutiques and online at www.petluvexpress.com

Many people enjoy celebrating special occasions, such as birthdays and holidays, with their dog. While giving your dog a gift is relatively straightforward (you buy her more of what she loves), the challenge has always been complementing the gift with a heartfelt card that your dog will appreciate. Hallmark doesn't make greeting cards for dogs. But Crunchkins has met this demand with innovative and patented greeting cards, called Crunch Cards, that are made from rawhide and are edible.

Crunch Cards were designed in conjunction with a veterinarian. Each card is flat, like cardboard, measures 4⅜ by 6⅛ inches, and is imprinted (using edible, nontoxic ink) with an adorable cartoon drawing and message. Each card is also packaged with a brightly colored paper envelope (for mailing) that's not edible (strictly speaking; many dogs do like to eat paper).

Crunchkins makes Crunch Cards for all types of special occasions and holidays. The cards are humorous and extremely cheerful. What your dog will appreciate most, however, is that they're edible and tasty.

Just Dogs Gourmet Biscuits, Cookies, and Treats

Price: Varies, based on quantity and product
Manufacturer: Just Dogs Gourmet
Phone: (888) 332-0307
Web site: www.justdogsgourmet.com
Availability: Online or at Just Dogs Gourmet mall kiosks nationwide

The next time you visit your favorite mall, you might discover a kiosk or store that sells freshly baked gourmet dog treats and biscuits. A handful of companies have opened locations in malls across the country, including Just Dogs Gourmet, which makes a line of gourmet biscuits and canine confections in a variety of flavors, shapes, and sizes.

Just Dogs Gourmet has more than thirty different treats, all made from natural ingredients, hand cut, and baked fresh in its own bakery, then shipped to the Just Dogs Gourmet franchisees, where the finishing touches, such as carob toppings, are added.

Just Dogs Gourmet can be expensive, but the company advertises that it uses only the best possible ingredients. Some of the most popular treat and biscuit flavors include: Chicken Fingers, Peppermint Bones, Pizza Bones, Cheddar Cheese Pretzels, Parmesan Twists, Bacon Pups, Peanut

Butter Banana Pinwheels, Healthy Hearts, Janie's Tailhouse Cookies, Mischief Munchies, and Carrot Crunchies. The Canine Confection treats are made from yogurt and carob.

Kong Stuff'N Hounds 27 Paste and Snaps

Price: Varies by product
Manufacturer: Kong Company
Phone: (303) 216-2626
Web site: www.kongcompany.com
Availability: Pet supply stores nationwide

One of the most popular rubber chew toys for dogs is the world-famous Kong (see chapter 6). To make this toy even more fun and enjoyable for your dog, the Kong Company has created a line of treats called Stuff'N, which can be placed inside the chew toy. For example, Hounds 27 is packaged like ketchup and is a tasty, pastelike snack that gets squeezed into the hollow insides of the Kong toy. There's also a canned paste product (available in two flavors) that can be squirted into the Kong. Finally, the "snaps" are small biscuits that can be inserted into Kongs.

Tip A preservative-free alternative to using the Stuff'N in the Kong toys is to buy all-natural peanut butter from your local supermarket and use it to stuff the Kong. Some dog owners then freeze the peanut butter in the Kong to create a special frozen treat for their pampered pooch.

Dogs will spend hours chewing, bouncing, and chasing the rubber Kong toys, and they'll also love using their tongues to taste the yummy treats you place inside them. Although the Stuff'N products do contain some preservatives and other chemicals, they're also fortified with vitamins and minerals.

3

Canine Couture

Your Dog Can Follow the Latest Fashion Trends

For decades, designers from New York, Hollywood, Paris, London, and Italy have been trendsetters in the latest fashions for people. With each new season comes new colors, patterns, designs, and styles. The canine fashion industry is no different. Many big-name clothing designers for people have begun designing high-end fashions for dogs, and numerous other designers have launched businesses catering exclusively to the fast-growing canine fashion industry.

If you want your dog to be on the cutting edge of fashion, you'll need a designer collar accented with fancy identification tags (see chapter 4), plus you'll need to dress him in outfits that, in many cases, are inspired by the very latest fashion trends for people. In fact, it's often possible to dress yourself in designer clothing and have a matching wardrobe for your pampered pooch.

Give Your Dog a Fashion Makeover

Let's face it: Dogs don't *need* to wear clothing. After all, most breeds have a full body of hair that can be professionally groomed to make them look beautiful, well kept, and extremely refined. Except for small dogs and those with a very short coat who go outside in the cold, few dogs truly need any clothing at all. Yet those who pamper their dogs often enjoy dressing them up in adorable outfits. Some dogs don't mind being dressed up and even enjoy this extra pampering, while other dogs quickly make it clear they're uncomfortable wearing clothes, no matter how fashionable they are. You must respect your dog's wishes in this matter.

When you go clothes shopping for your dog, you'll quickly discover you have a lot to choose from. You'll discover casual T-shirts for your pampered pooch, plus full outfits, dresses, coats, sweaters, jackets, sweatshirts, robes, pajamas, and even boots. Colorful bandanas also make wonderful canine fashion accessories.

Combine these fashion elements with designer collars, leashes, and ID tags (see chapter 4), along with bows and barrettes (if your dog has enough hair), and the fashion possibilities are endless. Plus, with each new season, the canine fashion industry introduces new designs.

Dressing your dog is one way to pamper him. But, it really caters to your own vanity and taste. So if you're going to make your dog a fashion icon, make sure you keep his comfort and safety in mind.

Quality Counts

Just as you wouldn't wear poorly made clothing or clothes that are uncomfortable, it's important to choose outfits and clothing items for your dog that not only look good, but are extremely comfortable and safe.

Aside from the clothing's appearance, here are some helpful guidelines:

✦ Choose outfits that are well made and fabrics that will be comfortable for your dog. Canine couture is made from a wide range of fabrics, including cotton, fleece, cashmere, wool, and polyester. Find outfits that are soft, durable, and odor free.

✦ Make sure the outfits you choose are the appropriate size; not too big and definitely not too small.

✦ Make sure the outfit contains no loose buttons, decorations, or other elements that could become a choking hazard.

✦ The outfit should in no way restrict your dog's movement or ability to breathe.

✦ Select clothing that's easy for you to put on and take off your dog. Clothing that uses Velcro or snaps, as opposed to buttons or zippers, is often easier.

✦ Keeping the clothing clean is important. Make sure you follow washing instructions for the clothing. Never use harsh detergents or cleaning products with chemicals that could be harmful to your dog. If an outfit needs to be dry-cleaned, find a dry cleaner that uses a chemical-free cleaning process.

Size Matters

Most canine fashions come in a variety of sizes to accommodate a broad range of dogs and breeds. Unfortunately, there are no industry standards when it comes to sizing, so you'll need to pay attention to the sizing guidelines offered by each designer or manufacturer.

To ensure a proper fit when buying canine clothes, you'll need to know the following information about your dog. Use a cloth tape measure.

◆ Your dog's length: measure along his back, from his neck to the beginning of his tail

◆ Your dog's neck: measure the circumference of your dog's neck

◆ Your dog's chest: measure the circumference of your dog's chest around his ribs, which tends to be the widest spot

You'll also want to know your dog's weight. Some dog clothing manufacturers base clothing sizes exclusively on weight. For example, a size "small" would fit dogs between 8 and 10 pounds, a size "medium" would fit dogs weighing between 12 and 14 pounds, while a size "large" would fit dogs between 16 and 22 pounds. However, this will vary greatly among manufacturers.

Some high-end canine fashion houses will custom-manufacture clothing for your dog. Exact measurements will then be necessary.

> *Tip* Clothing should never be too tight on your dog, especially around his neck or waist. If the fabric is not stretchy, make sure you add at least a quarter of an inch to the neck measurement and half an inch to the chest measurement to ensure a comfortable fit.

Couture for the Pampered Pooch

You can go to any pet supply store and find an assortment of T-shirts, dresses, and other inexpensive fashion options for your dog. These might cost anywhere from $5 to $25 per outfit. Truly pampered dogs, however, insist on only high-end designer fashions, where a doggy T-shirt can cost more than $100 and a complete outfit might cost $200 to $500, or more.

The following is information about a handful of popular designers who are pioneers in the fast-growing canine fashion industry. This, however, is only a small sample of the high-end fashion products available. To learn about other high-end designers, visit an upscale pet supply boutique, attend Pet Fashion Week (see the box on page 31), or read the latest issues of upscale dog magazines, such as *The New York Dog Magazine*, *The Hollywood Dog Magazine*, *Modern Dog*, *The Bark*, *Paw Luxuries*, or *WAG*, which are available at many newsstands.

Aurora Sheepskins

Price: $60 and up
Manufacturer: Aurora Sheepskin Pet Products
Phone: (954) 455-0405
Web site: www.aurorapetproducts.com
Availability: Online

Designed to keep your small dog warm, Aurora Sheepskin Pet Products has a collection of stylish leather and sheepskin coats in a variety of colors. Many of the coats have a D-ring on the back for a leash, so they double as a harness. All coats use large Velcro tabs (around the dog's neck area and waist) to fasten the coats securely. These coats are extremely elegant, and matching carriers, leashes, and collars are also available.

Burberry Dog Trench Coat

Price: $225
Manufacturer: Burberry
Phone: (866) 589-0499
Web site: www.burberry.com
Availability: Online and from Burberry stores nationwide

Inspired by the water-resistant, taupe, signature trench coats that Burberry has been selling for decades, the Burberry Dog Trench Coat (style no. 31404101) is made in Britain and is manufactured from a fine cotton fabric (with the signature check lining). It has a single leather-covered buckle that secures a belt that goes around the dog's waist. This stylish trench coat is available in three sizes. Similar styles are available for humans.

Friends of Babydoll Collection

Price: $290 to $530
Manufacturer: Donald J. Pliner
Phone: (888) 307-1630
Web site: www.donaldjpliner.com
Availability: Online and from the designer's stores

Fashion designer Donald J. Pliner is known for his luxurious fashions for men and women. He also offers his Friends of Babydoll Collection for well-dressed dogs. The collection includes fine leather jackets in a variety of styles, including the After Sport Leather Ski Jacket ($370), the Carolina Scarf Jacket ($290), and the Sporty Studded Jacket ($530). Each style is available in a variety of colors and sizes. Some styles are only available from Donald J. Pliner's retail showrooms in cities such as Beverly Hills, Las Vegas, and Coral Gables, Florida.

Fifi & Romeo

Price: $100 and up
Manufacturer: Fifi & Romeo
Phone: (323) 857-7215
Web site: www.fifiandromeo.com
Availability: Online or from the company's Hollywood, California, boutique

If you saw the movies *Legally Blond* and *Legally Blond 2*, where the main character's dog, Bruiser, wore a variety of designer outfits, you've already seen some of the canine couture designed by Fifi & Romeo. Their styles have also been seen on many television shows, including *The Simple Life* (with Paris Hilton and Nicole Richie) and *The Oprah Winfrey Show*, and on CNN, VH1, MTV, and E!. Many of the company's designs are also seen regularly in entertainment magazines where big-name celebrities are featured in photos with their dogs. Based in the heart of Hollywood, just blocks away from CBS Television Center, Fifi & Romeo boasts a large celebrity clientele.

Fifi & Romeo was launched in 1998 and has become a pioneer and world leader in high-end canine couture. Designer T-shirts (starting at $100), along with lovely handmade dresses and elaborately detailed outfits are available from the company's extremely upscale boutique, located at 7282 Beverly Boulevard in Los Angeles. It's well worth visiting the store if you're in the area. The company's web site also offers a selection of pieces from the ever-changing Fifi & Romeo collection. Most of the clothing is handmade in a manufacturing facility located directly above the boutique. This enables the company to accommodate custom orders.

> ## Hot Debuts at Pet Fashion Week
>
> Just as all of the world's biggest designers gather once a year in New York and Europe for Fashion Week to showcase the latest styles and fashions for people, starting in August 2006, Pet Fashion Week (www.petfashionweek.com) in New York City became an annual event for upscale canine fashion designers to show off their latest styles. This is the ultimate event for people to discover the latest, most fashionable and fabulous ways to pamper their dogs.

The Gilded Paw

Price: $25 to $300
Manufacturer: The Gilded Paw
Phone: (888) 509-8752
Web site: www.thegildedpaw.com
Availability: Online

The Gilded Paw is one of many upscale pet boutiques that offer a large selection of high-end canine couture from a variety of designers. Many of the fashions are handmade from fine fabrics. Some of the company's popular items include faux fur coats, polar fleece hooded sweatshirts, T-shirts, sport jerseys, and formal dresses. This is the place where owners of well-dressed male and female dogs shop.

Gucci

Price: $80 to $235 and up
Manufacturer: Gucci
Phone: (212) 826-2600 (New York) or (310) 278-3451 (Beverly Hills)
Web site: www.gucci.com
Availability: Online and from Gucci stores nationwide

In addition to lovely collars, identification tags, and a luxurious carrier, Gucci offers a selection of canine cotton sweaters in a variety of colors and sizes ($235 and up) that feature the embroidered Gucci logo. The Gucci dog bandana, with signature web necktie ($80), has the company's signature beige and ebony "GG" fabric with an attached green-red-green signature collar.

House of Canine Couture

Price: $30 to $300
Manufacturer: House of Canine Couture
Phone: (866) 745-0512
Web site: www.caninecouture.ca
Availability: Online

Offering four lines—Silver Label, Street, Sport, and Spa—House of Canine Couture makes custom-fitted clothing that's fashionable, trendy, and extremely elegant. Within the Silver Label line, you'll find a selection of hand-sewn faux fur coats. Each coat is made to order and has a satin lining. The Street collection includes an assortment of designer coats and rain gear, while the Sport line includes jackets and suits made from fleece and other fabrics.

The Spa line has robes, sweatshirts, and bodysuits designed for the ultimate in comfort and high fashion. All the clothing sold by House of Canine Couture is well made, yet reasonably priced. Most designs come in a variety of sizes and colors, or are custom-made for your dog.

Louisdog

Price: $35 to $94
Manufacturer: Louisdog
Web site: www.louisdog.com
Availability: Upscale canine boutiques nationwide

Louisdog sells luxurious cashmere sweaters, plus a collection of matching toys, blankets, and dog beds.

Louisdog makes a large selection of dog beds, blankets, and toys made of ultrasoft and extremely plush cotton and polyester materials. Most of Louisdog's products come in pastel shades of blue, yellow, and pink.

These design elements have been carried over to the company's canine clothing line, which includes a variety of T-shirts, dresses, and extremely cute cashmere sweaters (suitable for male and female dogs). The Louisdog collection caters mainly to small dogs and puppies. Many of the fabrics used are stretchable to ensure a perfect fit.

Bark Jacobs

Price: $150 to $175
Manufacturer: Marc Jacobs
Phone: (212) 343-1490
Web site: www.marcjacobs.com
Availability: Marc Jacobs stores

Fashion designer Marc Jacobs not only creates fashions for men and women, but under his Bark Jacobs line he sells a selection of classy yet simple dog sweaters. They're available in poppy (red), brume (blue), and cruso (gray).

Nicole Miller

Price: Under $30
Manufacturer: Nicole Miller
Phone: (212) 288-9779
Web site: www.nicolemiller.com or www.petco.com
Availability: Pet supply superstores nationwide, including PetCo.

Offering a variety of collars, bandanas, shirts, and other fashionable items, designer Nicole Miller brings her unique patterns and prints to canine fashions that are affordable and are available at pet supply superstores nationwide. The Nicole Miller Mesh Vest, for example, has a matching leash and collar (sold separately). The vest itself is a sporty yet comfortable mesh design that uses a reflective silver trim, a full-front opening with Velcro closure, and an accessory pouch on the back. The buttonhole at the neckline lets you attach a leash to your dog's collar through the back of the vest. The vest is available in three sizes.

Polo Ralph Lauren

Price: $32 to $95
Manufacturer: Polo Ralph Lauren
Phone: (888) 475-7674
Web site: www.polo.com
Availability: Online

Available in nine colors (which coordinate perfectly with Polo's fashions for people), Polo Ralph Lauren sells a luxurious and sleeveless cashmere sweater for dogs ($95). The sweater is knit with the company's signature cabling along the back and has a clean rib stitch on the underside. It's finished with a ribbed collar and a convenient opening at the back of the neck for a leash.

For preppy dogs, the company offers a collection of classic cotton-mesh, short-sleeve Polo shirts in five colors ($32 each). These shirts are designed with classic Polo details, including a ribbed collar, two-button placket, and banded short sleeves. Each shirt sports the embroidered Polo logo, in a contrasting color, on the collar.

Polo Ralph Lauren's dog clothing is only available online from the company's web site. Click on the "Gifts" icon, followed by the "For the Pup" icon to find the latest canine fashions. Matching Polo shirts for men and women are also available.

Roxy Hunt Couture

Price: $18.99 to $72.99
Manufacturer: Roxy Hunt Couture
Phone: (877) 476-9948
Web site: www.roxyhuntcouture.com
Availability: Online and from upscale canine boutiques nationwide

Millions of people watched actress Crystal Hunt play the character Lizzie Spaulding on the popular CBS soap opera *Guiding Light*. She has also starred in a handful of movies, including *The Derby Stallion, From Earth to the Moon,* and *Problem Child II.* In addition to being a beautiful young actress, Crystal is a dog lover. She can often be seen toting around Roxy, an adorable Maltese who is the inspiration behind Roxy Hunt Couture.

Hunt's goal has been to create a classy and well-made line of canine couture, but to offer each outfit at an affordable price. The designs are all manufactured in the United States using fine fabrics.

Originally launched in autumn 2005, Roxy Hunt Couture is designed by Hunt. "I have been acting for most of my life. When I started appearing with my dog Roxy on *Guiding Light,* she'd often be wearing outfits I created for her. Fans of the show started writing letters asking where they could purchase similar outfits, so I established Roxy Hunt Couture," says Hunt.

The collection changes every season but always offers well-made, trendy designs inspired by the latest fashions for people. The collection includes several dresses and coats for female dogs, plus a stunning and highly detailed tuxedo and sailor's shirt for male dogs.

Give your pampered pooch a touch of international style with Roxy Hunt Couture's Frenchy Striped Tee design. The $42.99 outfit includes the blouse, skirt, and matching beret. The blouse comes in a blue-and-white or red-and-white stripe.

This fancy black tuxedo from Roxy Hunt Couture has an interchangeable "shirt and tie" to create a variety of formal looks. This outfit is ideal for weddings and other fancy occasions.

The blue-and-white-striped sailor's shirt from Roxy Hunt Couture is fashionable yet casual. As with all the company's designs, it includes a themed charm around the neck area.

The Sleepy Bed Blankie Set has a unisex design and includes pajamas, plus a matching pillow and blanket, all made from an incredibly soft, pastel-colored fleece. The pajamas are available in lavender and aqua blue with yellow trim and are machine washable.

"My designs are inspired by the latest fashions for people. My ideas come from outfits that I'd wear myself, both on *Guiding Light* and in my everyday life. In addition to the line of clothes we've already released, in 2006 and 2007 we'll be releasing hoodies, inspired by the Juicy Couture hoodies, with faux fur collars. All of my designs for female dogs are very girly."

One thing that sets Roxy Hunt Couture apart from other canine clothing lines is that each outfit incorporates some type of themed charm around the neck area. For example, the company's blue-and-white-striped Sailor's Tee has a nautical charm.

"I try to ensure my clothing will hold up better than other clothing people buy for their dogs," says Hunt. "I want my designs to be elegant, classy, and durable. Even after many washings, I want my clothes to be as pretty as the day they were bought. I have bought so many expensive outfits for my dog that were poorly made and that didn't hold up, which was disappointing. I want dog owners and their dogs to really like the outfits we offer through Roxy Hunt Couture."

When choosing fashions for your dog, Hunt advises, "Choose clothing that accentuates your dog's coloring. If your dog is white, choose bright colored clothes or solid black, for example. For dogs with darker hair, I like clothing that features browns and blacks, plus dual-tones."

Hunt says Roxy loves dressing up. "Never force your dog to wear clothing if she appears uncomfortable."

Hunt is thrilled to have her dog clothing sold at upscale pet supply stores throughout the country, but her dream is to open her own Roxy Hunt Couture boutique and to have her clothes also sold in Neiman Marcus stores. So far, the most exciting thing that's happened since launching her clothing line has been to have her fashions shown at the Westminster Dog Show.

To spoil her dog, Hunt says, "I only feed Roxy the best quality food. I also have five or six beds for her around the house. While people say it's not good to feed your dog too many bones and treats, I always reward her with them. Wherever you look around my house, you'll find Roxy's toys and treats everywhere. I swear she doesn't even know she's a dog. She's so pampered."

Any dog will snuggle up comfortably in Roxy Hunt Couture's incredibly soft pajamas. They're available in a feminine lavender color and an aqua blue.

Scooter's Friends

Price: $50 and up
Manufacturer: Scooter's Friends
Phone: (312) 718-3359
Web site: www.scootersfriends.com
Availability: Online and from upscale canine boutiques nationwide

Designer coats for small dogs are the focus of Scooter's Friends. The company uses a selection of faux furs, leather, vinyl, wool, and corduroy to create its line of elegant winter and all-weather coats. Matching blankets are also available.

"I saw the need for stylish, but affordable dog apparel. And living in Chicago, where the winters are long, I wanted outerwear that was warm and durable, but looked good too! So bringing a quality line of dog apparel to fashion-forward, value-conscious people seemed to make sense," says the company's founder, Kathy Stevens.

Your dog will leave home in style when he dresses in one of the designer coats from Scooter's Friends.

Inspired by today's top designers, Scooter's Friends offers a wide array of apparel, ranging from hip corduroy jackets to classic wool tweeds, to sleek wet looks, to mink-trimmed coats. Sizing is generous for a comfortable fit for dogs of all breeds, shapes, and sizes.

The Toby Line

Price: $59.99 to $79.99
Manufacturer: The Toby Line
Phone: (404) 408-1967
Web site: www.thetobyline.com
Availability: Online

Offering luxurious designs made from fine fabrics, the Toby Line has reversible coats in more than a dozen styles. The current collection includes rich brocade, soft corduroy, handsome tweed, ultra-suede,

Fashion Follows Function

Some outfits can be both fashionable and functional. Many coats, for example, are waterproof (or at least water-resistant), enabling your dog to stay dry in the rain or snow. There are also wool and fleece coats that will keep your pooch warm.

For the ultimate in weather protection, booties for dogs are available from a variety of manufacturers. DogBooties.com (218-727-3121; www.dogbooties.com), for example, specializes in all-weather boots for dogs of all sizes and breeds. When shopping for booties, focus on the quality of materials used, warmth, water resistance, and durability. Remember, most booties are designed to be used outdoors only to protect your dog from the harsh elements while on a walk. Dogs are not meant to wear shoes (or boots) throughout the day. To protect your dog's paws, if the insides of the booties get wet, remove them immediately and allow them to dry.

and classic bouclé. According to the company, each jacket is designed to offer quality, a unique design, and the ultimate in comfort.

The company also makes a collection of colorful Lycra jackets in ten styles, designed to showcase your pampered pooch's unique personality. Each Toby garment is fashioned with ease of use in mind. All closures use Velcro, with the occasional button added for decoration. Outerwear is created with ready holes for harnesses as well as leashes. And most of the styles are reversible.

Dressing Up Your Dog for the Holidays

Whether you're looking for the perfect formal gown or suit for your dog to wear to Christmas dinner, or you'll be attending a Halloween costume party with your dog, there are a few companies that offer fun, comical, and inexpensive costumes exclusively for dogs.

Especially right after a visit to the groomer, rain gear for dogs will help keep your pampered pooch dry. This raincoat will be available from Pets at Play (866-PLAY-PACK; www.petsatplay.com) starting in late 2006. It comes in a variety of sizes and colors, and has a handy storage pocket on the side.

Glamourdog

Price: $26 and up
Manufacturer: Glamourdog
Phone: (877) 452-6364
Web site: www.glamourdog.com/costumes.html
Availability: Online

This online boutique has a collection of fun Halloween costumes for your pampered pooch. Some of the dozens of costumes include a fairy princess, pirate, bunny rabbit, bumblebee, football player, pumpkin, lady bug, cheerleader, and pig. The costumes come in a variety of sizes. Some, however, are more suitable specifically for smaller or larger dogs.

Happy Paws Pet Clothes

Price: $20 to $40
Manufacturer: Happy Paws Pet Clothes
Phone: (574) 370-2256
Web site: www.happypawsdaycare.com
Availability: Online

Happy Paws Pet Clothes sells a large collection of canine fashions, including a selection of holiday-themed outfits for male and female dogs. Many of these outfits are ideal for holiday get-togethers, formal dinners, and even cocktail parties. But remember, no matter how well trained he is, your dog can't be your designated driver.

Who's the Leader of the Club That's Made for You and Me?

Traveling to Walt Disney World Resort in Orlando, Florida, for vacation but can't bring your dog? Consider bringing home a Disney souvenir canine T-shirt, or one of the other official Disney Tails products designed for pets. There's also a popular Mickey Mouse–shaped personalized dog tag made from metal that can be custom engraved. These products are sold at various shops throughout the Disney theme parks, plus at the Disney Tails store in Downtown Disney.

Currently available exclusively at the Roosevelt Field Mall in Garden City, New York, the Han Nari store has a wide range of fashionable, adorable, and high-quality Disney-themed dog clothing imported from Japan. For details, log on to www.creativeyoko.co.jp/hannari/top.htm or call the Han Nari store at (516) 742-4034.

Casual Canine

Price: $20 to $40
Manufacturer: Pet Edge
Phone: (800) 738-3343
Web site: www.petedge.com
Availability: Online from Pet Edge and from pet supply stores nationwide

Casual Canine sells dozens of humorous and inexpensive Halloween costumes for dogs of all sizes and breeds. You can dress your dog up as a hot dog (with ketchup or mustard), or choose from a clown, bumblebee, or princess costume, for example. The company also has a fashionable wedding dress and coordinating tux, plus a selection of Christmas-themed outfits, such as Santa hats and reindeer antlers.

4

Collars, Tags, and Leashes

Show Off Your Dog's Unique Style

*D*esigner collars, handmade identification tags, collar charms, and leashes that are highly functional yet unique are what today's trendy dogs are all excited to be wearing. (Okay, it's really more the dog owners who get excited, but nevertheless, these are the popular items worn by pampered pooches everywhere.)

Your dog's collar basically serves three purposes. You can attach a leash and walk him. It can be a place to hang your dog's identification tags. And it can make a fashion statement. For designer collars and leashes, dog owners can turn to familiar names such as Gucci, Coach, and Burberry. For the ultimate in high-fashion collars, though, look to companies such as Posh Pooch and Twil Animal, which sell handmade designer collars that range in price from $500 to $2,500.

Many of these items are also on the cutting edge of fashion, designed to coordinate perfectly with what even the trendiest celebrities in New York, Los Angeles, and Paris are wearing. One thing you can be sure of is that you won't find many of the products in this chapter at your local pet supply superstore. Some are even too exclusive for the most prestigious pet boutiques, and are available only by setting up a private appointment with the designer.

In this chapter, you'll also learn about a few collars that use the latest wireless communications and GPS technology to help keep you in touch with your dog, while other collars, tags, and leashes you'll be reading about are handmade from fine leathers, exotic skins, gold, silver, platinum, and diamonds, and are one-of-a-kind. Combine a designer collar with a matching leash, add a unique ID tag, and you're well on your way to showing the world just how pampered your pooch really is.

Designer Collars and Leashes

Discover how something as simple as a strip of leather, cloth, or nylon that goes around your dog's neck can be transformed into the ultimate fashion statement. Here's a small sampling of what's available when it comes to designer collars and leashes.

Twil Animal

Price: $1,500 to $2,500
Manufacturer: Twil Animal
Phone: (646) 261-9703
E-mail: twilanimal@aol.com
Availability: By appointment only

These collars, handmade made in Padova, Italy, by Twil Animal, are special in several ways. Each collar is made from fine leathers and other high-quality materials and is one of a limited edition. Beyond that, each incorporates Space-Age Reflector (SAR) material in its design. This reflective material will help your dog be seen by oncoming traffic, day or night. Each collar is also designed based on a personality type, so dogs and their owners can make a fashion statement that perfectly suits them.

According to Willis (he goes by just one name, like Versace), the company's CEO, "The Twil Animal line was created to safeguard the wearer. Our collars are unique. We combine high fashion with animal safety. Italian leather, suede, nubuck, and SAR materials are used to create a timeless fashion statement."

The SAR material is a highly reflective material composed of crushed particles. The small particles act like little mirrors. When any type of light hits them, they reflect the light, giving the collar a glistening diamond look during the day and at night. "Every year, millions of dogs are killed accidentally by automobiles," says Willis. "SAR material incorporated into each collar design will give your pet a chance to be visible at all times. Plus, it's very posh."

Collar designs in the Twil Animal product line go from basic to extravagant, and, like all high fashion, the available styles change every year. In 2005, Twil Animal sold out its first collar collection, which was available exclusively in Europe. In 2006, the new product line was made available in America for the first time, although the collars are not sold in stores or online. Twil Animal collars can only be special ordered by contacting the company directly.

"We discovered each pet takes on more than 60 percent of their owner's personality," says Willis. "That being said, we design our collars for every lifestyle. When you look at the Twil Animal product line, you will see designs that cater to all personalities. Our collars are designed to fit dogs of all sizes and breeds. My inspiration for each collar design comes from the many personalities I continue to encounter. It's truly amazing to see multiple dogs from the same breed, each with vastly different personalities."

Since Twil Animal caters exclusively to an upscale clientele, the company only sells directly to its clients. Each collar is part of a limited edition, which adds to the exclusivity of the product line. "We make 5,000 pieces a year," says Willis. "We want to keep our relationship with clients very personal. I speak to each and every client we sell to."

Several thicknesses (1-inch, 1 ½-inch, and 2-inch) are available in most styles. Once the dog owner chooses a collar style, each is custom-fitted for the dog. No matter what type of collar you choose for your dog, Willis says, "You must try it on the pet to be absolutely sure of a perfect fit." Only a limited number of each style collar are manufactured worldwide, ensuring that dog owners are able to purchase a collar that's truly exclusive.

Twil Animal's Invecchiato (bottom) and Costolato (top) collar designs, released in 2006. They're available in several colors, including chocolate, pink, black, tan, and nochola.

In addition to its line of upscale collars, which are priced at $1,500 each, the company offers an even more exclusive couture line. "I will sit down and observe the animal's activity with the owner for several days. From this observation, I will design three to five collars for the pet," Willis explains. "The designs can go from mild to wild, depending on the pet and owner's personality and lifestyle. The Twil Animal couture line starts at $2,500 per collar."

Starting in mid-2006, Twil Animal will be making leashes to match its exclusive line of collars.

Posh Pooch

Price: $100 to $795
Manufacturer: Posh Pooch
Phone: (917) 371-8020
Web site: www.posh-pooch.com
Availability: Online and from select upscale stores

Designed by Giannci Genau, president and lead designer at New York–based Posh Pooch, each collar and leash offered by the company coordinates with one or more of Posh Pooch's handmade dog carriers or purses (see chapter 8)—although they make incredible fashion statements all by themselves.

Like Posh Pooch's carriers, what sets these collars and leashes apart is that they're manufactured in Italy using fine leathers and exotic animal skins such as stingray, python, crocodile, and alligator. Each collar and leash is sold separately. They're available in a variety of sizes and trendy colors. Styles, colors, and designs change each season. Leashes are either 4 or 6 feet long and have solid brass hardware.

Coach Mini Signature Collar and Leash

Price: $68 each
Manufacturer: Coach
Phone: (888) 262-6224
Web site: www.coach.com
Availability: Online and from Coach stores

Coach leather products, including the company's handbags and purses, have a unique fashion look that's known around the world. That same quality and appearance have been incorporated into several styles of dog collars and leashes.

Tip In past years, Coach has released other collars and leashes in different designs and color schemes. They can still be found at some Coach stores and through online auction web sites such as eBay.

The Mini Signature Dog Collar with Charms (style no. 8837), for example, is available in ¾-inch and 1-inch widths and four lengths. The collar features Coach's signature fabric with leather trim, a Coach logo nickel hangtag (which can be engraved on the back), and a khaki and red enamel heart charm. Available in two color schemes (silver/khaki/red and khaki/fuchsia), this is a classy-looking collar that's ideal for female dogs and owners who want a Coach collar to coordinate with their own Coach products.

The matching Coach Mini Signature Leash (style no. 8838) also has Coach's signature fabric and leather trim. The 52-inch leash is available in ½-inch and 1-inch widths.

For male dogs, Coach sells a classic black calfskin collar with an enamel and nickel bone charm and nickel Coach logo roller buckle ($42, style no. 4000). It's available in two widths and five lengths. A red version of the collar has a heart-shaped charm. A matching 52-inch leash is available ($58, style no. 4004).

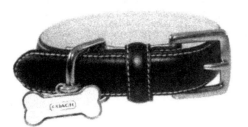

Coach makes a variety of collar styles for pampered pooches, including this black calfskin collar with an enamel and nickel bone charm and nickel Coach logo roller buckle, which is perfect for the smaller boys.

Patent Leather Collection

Price: Varies
Manufacturer: Rouge New York
Phone: (866) 523-7168
Web site: www.rougenewyork.com
Availability: Online and from upscale canine boutiques

These designer collars are made from Brazilian leather and have custom-made buckles. The collars have a timeless, classic, and elegant design for male or female dogs of any size and breed. They're available in pink, baby blue, red, and lime green and come in a variety of sizes and widths.

Les Poochs Collars and Leashes

Price: $800 to $1,000
Manufacturer: LesPoochs.com, Inc.
Phone: (800) 745-4512
Web site: www.lespoochs.com
Availability: Online and from the company's boutiques in New York, Paris, and London

Burberry for Dogs

Periodically, Burberry, another popular designer of clothing and accessories for people, releases various dog accessories and clothing items. In the past, several collars and leashes have been offered as limited-edition, seasonal items. For details, check with your local Burberry store, the company's web site (www.burberry.com), or eBay.

The collars and matching leashes sold by Les Poochs are beautiful, extravagant, and extremely classy. Made from fine Italian leather, genuine ostrich, and alligator, the collars have a patented, twist Click N'Lock mechanism (instead of a traditional buckle). This unique closure is made from aluminum and titanium, making it lightweight, extremely durable, comfortable for the dog, and easy for you to open and close.

Every collar in the collection is custom-made to your dog's exact measurements. Collars are available in black, red, or yellow, and each is accompanied by an 18-karat white gold identification tag. Every matching leash (sold separately) is custom made to your specifications and comfort. Les Poochs also makes a selection of other high-end products, including carriers, dog beds, and professional grooming tools.

GoTags Personalized Collars

Price: $15.95
Manufacturer: GoTags.com
Phone: (866) 369-4169
Web site: www.gotags.com
Availability: Online

These custom-embroidered or embossed nylon and leather collars are available in eight colors, in lengths between 10 inches and 26 inches, and three widths. Each collar can be customized with your dog's name and phone number, so you don't need an ID tag. The collars have polished stainless steel buckles and are extremely durable. Matching leashes, which can also be custom embroidered, are available, too.

Pick of the Glitter Swarovski Crystal Collars

Price: $98 to $140
Manufacturer: Pick of the Glitter Fine Jewelry
Phone: (800) 717-2709
Web site: www.petglitter.com
Availability: Online

Artist and jewelry maker Rachael Poole has created a line of more than 20 stunning collars and collar charms, all of which feature genuine Austrian Swarovski crystals. Each collar is handmade and customized for the dog. These collars come in a variety of colors. Most are more suitable for female dogs, due to their color and sparkle, but several of the designs can proudly be worn by male dogs.

The collars are made to order, based on your dog's neck measurements, and each is also adjustable up to 1 inch.

Pick of the Glitter sells a beautiful selection of custom, handmade collars that feature genuine Austrian Swarovski crystals.

The crystal collars function as collars, but look more like jewelry. Poole also makes a lovely Puppy Love Crystal Collar, which is really a thin crystal necklace that's complemented with a crystal heart charm. It's perfect for pampered puppies.

To match any of her collars, Poole has crystal collar charms made with the dog's birthstone. Each charm is mounted in a sterling silver setting and comes with a clip so it can be easily and securely attached to any collar.

Because each collar is custom-made, allow one to two weeks for delivery. Each collar comes in a velvet-lined gift box. If you can't afford a genuine diamond necklace for your pampered pooch, the Pick of the Glitter crystal collars offer plenty of sparkle, plus a true touch of class.

Crystal collar charms from Pick of the Glitter can include your dog's birthstone, and add a touch of elegance and sparkle.

A Tail We Could Wag Collars and Leashes

Price: $24 to $29 for collars; $29 to $34 for leashes
Manufacturer: A Tail We Could Wag
Phone: (208) 726-1763
Web site: www.tailwags.com
Availability: Online

These collars and matching leashes come in more than a dozen designs. They are extremely colorful, and are made from top-quality bridle leather. Each is nicely accented with the company's exclusive hand-woven fabric. The threads are intricately woven, creating a look that is truly unique. For dog owners, belts that nicely match the weave designs of the collars and leashes are available. The stainless steel hardware has a contemporary look.

Much of the inspiration for these collar and leash designs comes from the artistry of the Maya people of Guatemala. The Maya are skilled artists who have been expertly weaving cotton goods for centuries. The colors and designs they use are inspired by their unique heritage and culture.

Life Is Good

Price: $20 for collars; $22 to $25 for leashes
Manufacturer: Life Is Good
Phone: (888) 878-2987
Web site: www.lifeisgood.com
Availability: Online and from Life Is Good stores

Life Is Good dog collars and leashes are fun and upbeat.

There's nothing exotic, fancy, or extravagant about these collars and leashes; they're simply fun and offer a positive and upbeat message. The Life Is Good brand sells a wide range of clothing and accessories for people, and also has matching collars, leashes, flying discs, bowls, and balls for dogs. These products all include the message "life is good," plus the adorable corporate icon, which happens to be a dog.

The collars and leashes are made from comfortable, durable, and washable nylon fabric. The graphics are woven into ribbons and sewn down into the collars and leashes, which are available in a variety of sizes and colors.

Earth Dog Collars

Price: $19 to $24
Manufacturer: Earth Dog
Phone: (877) 654-5528
Web site: www.earthdog.com
Availability: Online

Earth Dog's goal is to create ecoconscious products that dogs and people both will love. To that end, they've created a line of comfortable dog collars and matching leashes that are made from hemp. According to the company, "Our collars, leashes, and couplers feature triple-layer, 100% hemp canvas construction; contoured, quick release hardware and the most distinctive, quality trimmings available. Unlike nylon and other synthetics, hemp softens with wear, making these collars extremely comfortable for your dog, and because they're machine-washable, they're hassle-free."

Earth Dog collars are available in fifteen colorful styles that enable your dog to showcase her personality. They come in two widths (¾-inch and 1-inch) and are top quality, yet competitively priced.

Collars with a High-Tech Twist

For dogs who tend to get loose a lot, or for owners who are obsessed with knowing where their dog is and what she's doing throughout the day, two high-tech collars are available that use the latest wireless communication and GPS technologies.

Global Pet Finder

Price: $349
Manufacturer: GPS Tracks, LLC
Phone: (516) 938-2121
Web site: www.globalpetfinder.com
Availability: Online and from upscale canine boutiques

This high-tech collar has a built-in global positioning system (GPS), enabling you to pinpoint your dog's exact location any time and anywhere in the United States and many parts of the world. If your dog gets loose often by sneaking out the front door or escaping from her fenced-in play area, this is the perfect solution for tracking her down fast.

Using any computer that's connected to the Internet, the Global Pet Finder system enables you to create a virtual perimeter around an area and will notify you immediately if the dog leaves it. Whenever your dog is wearing the collar, if she wanders outside the virtual boundary you have set up, you'll be alerted immediately and continuously sent the exact location of your pet using a two-way wireless device, such as a cell phone, PDA, or computer. (Keep in mind, the Global Pet Finder is *not* meant to be a restraining, containment, or training device. It will, however, help you track your dog's location.)

Unlike underground pet fence products, this one does *not* shock or harm the dog in any way if she leaves the designated area. Instead, the collar will send you an alert and enable you to track her.

The Global Pet Finder has a GPS that attaches to a dog's collar. You can then track your dog's exact location using any two-way wireless device, such as a cell phone, PDA, or computer.

If you have a dog who spends a lot of time outdoors, perhaps in your fenced yard, the Global Pet Finder collar also tracks the current temperature and will alert you if it gets too hot or cold for your dog's safety and comfort. The system requires no installation. The water-resistant unit simply attaches to your medium or large dog's collar. Within minutes after setting up the service, you'll never have to worry about your dog getting lost again.

Hear Now Collar

Price: $179.95
Manufacturer: The Hear Now
Phone: (866) 343-HEAR
Web site: www.thehearnow.com
Availability: Online and from select pet supply boutiques

This is a two-way pet communication system designed to keep you in touch with your pampered pooch, especially if she tends to get loose often. The fully waterproof and patented collar unit has a GPS tracking system and comes with a two-way walkie-talkie device that enables you to track your dog and even speak with her within a 12-mile radius. The collar also has built-in LED lights, so it's highly visible at night.

Not Your Typical Leashes

In addition to standard leashes, you'll find a variety of unusual designs that serve a variety of functions. FlexiUSA retractable leashes (800-543-4921; www.flexiusa.com) are a favorite among many dog owners because they give your dog freedom to move around as they extend to a length of up to 26 feet. They also offer the dog walker easy, one-handed control. These leashes come in five styles and several colors. They're available at most pet supply stores.

The WackyWalk'r (610-222-0679; www.wackywalkr.com) is a rubber leash that's designed to take the stress out of walking your dog, especially when she pulls. This leash is available in more than a dozen colors and stretches to twice its original length, while always keeping the dog walker in control. The two WackyWalk'r leash designs are available in four sizes and range in price from $23 to $29. Although the stretchy rubber design of these leashes may seem a bit odd, they offer excellent functionality.

The Bamboo Quick Control collar (877-224-PETS; www.bamboopet.com) has a built-in leash and has totally redesigned how a collar and leash combo can work together to benefit the dog and her owner. For the dog walker, this product offers a padded handle and a high-performance elastic band that connects to the attached collar. The collar is made from a soft yet strong nylon, with an equally strong metal buckle. Combined into one piece, the collar, leash, and handle give the dog walker maximum control. The product comes in five colors and several sizes. It's available at upscale pet supply stores nationwide, or directly from the company's web site.

Consider a Harness

An alternative to a collar is a harness. A harness wraps around your dog's body and evenly distributes the pressure caused by tugs on the leash. For small dogs and slender ones, a body harness is usually much safer than attaching a leash to an around-the-neck collar.

Hug-A-Dog Harness

Price: $24.95 to $52.95
Manufacturer: Hug-A-Dog
Phone: (800) 444-9475
Web site: www.hug-a-dog.com
Availability: Online

Hug-A-Dog manufactures dog harnesses that are custom-made to your dog's specific measurements. They come in a variety of fabrics, including reflective and water-resistant fabric or mesh, enabling you to custom-design harnesses with vastly different looks and functionality.

Unlike many other harnesses, the Hug-A-Dog attaches to your dog in seconds using Velcro straps (which wrap around the dog's waist and neck). There are no straps to untangle, and you never have to worry about matching up holes in the harness with your dog's neck and legs. For a few dollars extra, a special strap can be added, making the harness easy to attach directly to a car's seatbelt to safely secure your dog while you're driving.

Hug-A-Dog harnesses are well made and durable. They're ideal for very small to midsize dogs. The only drawback to the design is the nylon safety strap and plastic latch, which also goes around the dog's neck. If your dog has a chewing problem, she might be tempted to chew through this plastic latch, rendering it useless and creating a potential choking hazard. Never leave your dog unattended when she's wearing this type of harness.

Harness Play Pack

Price: $32.95 to $45.95
Manufacturer: Pets-at-Play
Phone: (866) PLAY-PACK
Web site: www.petsatplay.com
Availability: Online and from upscale canine boutiques nationwide

Nancy Kerrigan (not the figure skater) invented both the Sleep-N-Store dog bed (see chapter 5) and the patented Harness Play Pack, which is available for any size and breed of dog. The Harness Play Pack is a harness with extras: It has built-in pockets that hold a water bottle, flying disc toy (which doubles as

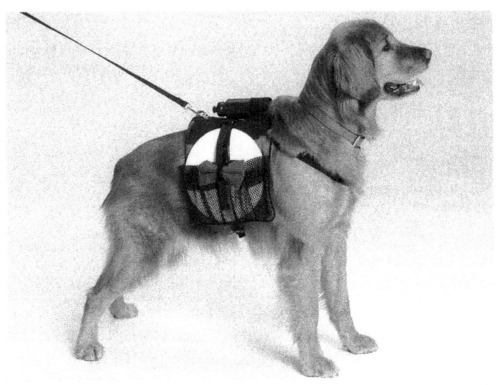

Everything you and your dog need for a fun time outside is built right into the Harness Play Pack.

a water dish), and a supply of disposable poop pick-up bags. The larger harnesses (for medium and large dogs) also come with a ball and extra pockets to store other small items, such as your keys.

Basically, the Harness Play Pack is designed to hold everything you'll need to spend a few minutes or several hours outside playing with your dog. Each of the harnesses' pockets stays closed using a Velcro tab. The harness also has a built-in, detachable leash although you can also use your own leash.

The Harness Play Pack comes in a variety of colors and sizes. Each harness is made of a cotton and polyester blend fabric, which balances comfort with durability. This product has received awards for its unique design.

Bella Paris Harnesses

Price: $34 to $36
Manufacturer: Bella Paris Pet Couture and Travel
Phone: (818) 823-3969
Web site: www.bellaparis.com
Availability: Online and from upscale canine boutiques nationwide

Bella Paris full-body harnesses come in a variety of designer fabrics and five sizes. For female dogs, the company also has a lovely line of harness dresses, adorned with bows and other decorative elements. For example, the Bella Butterfly harness dress is accented by a pink-sequined butterfly applique. This dress is made of a lightweight, lilac-colored, cotton fabric with bright pink trim and comes with a matching pink bow. The 1-inch ruffle adds to the harness' feminine look.

These harness dresses give the illusion of a dress, but are as comfortable and practical as any other harness vest. According to the Bella Paris web site, "These easy on and easy off Bella Paris harness vests are a comfortable alternative to using a collar on your little dog. It is recommended by veterinarians to avoid using a collar on smaller breeds. The tendency for these pups to develop tracheal problems from using a collar is higher since they have such delicate tracheas. These harness vests take the pressure off the throat of your pup and will disburse the pressure evenly throughout the chest area."

The harness vest closes with strong Velcro straps, so it stays secure and is easy to put on and take off in a hurry. The built-in D-ring on the back of each harness vest makes it easy to attach your dog's leash. The result is a design that is practical yet fashionable.

Just for Small Dogs

For smaller dogs, Cloak & Dawggie (212-594-3800; www.cloakanddawggie.com) makes a collection of full-body fabric harnesses in a wide range of colorful styles and patterns, including mesh. These harnesses easily pass for designer outfits, yet function as durable harnesses, complete with a leash hook on the back and easy-on/easy-off Velcro closures. Prices start at $68. These are among the nicest and classiest harnesses you'll find for small dogs.

ID Tags

Your dog's identification tag is extremely important. If she ever gets lost, whoever finds her can use the information on the tag to contact you. You want the tag to display your dog's name and your home and cell phone numbers. If there's room, it should also include your full address.

Tip Puttining your cell phone number on your dog's tag is especially important if you travel with your dog. Then, no matter where you are, someone who finds your dog will be able to reach you quickly.

Of course, you can go to any pet supply shop and spend between $5 and $10 to have an inexpensive metal or plastic ID tag engraved with your personal information. These tags are certainly practical, but they're not necessarily fashionable. The ID tags in this section are handmade works of art that fit nicely on any dog's collar, and prominently display your dog's name and your pertinent contact information. You're about to discover that a dog's ID tag can become a fine piece of jewelry that your pampered pooch will wear proudly (or at the very least, you'll be proud to have your dog wear).

Sally Harrell Dog Tags

Price: $37 to $40
Manufacturer: Sally Harrell
Phone: (619) 298-2983
Web site: www.SallyHarrell.net
Availability: Online

Sally Harrell is a metalsmith, jewelry designer, and dog lover from Charlotte, North Carolina. Combining her artistic skills with her love for animals, Harrell designed a line of handmade dog tags that were initially inspired by her own black Labrador Retriever puppy. In 2005, Harrell launched a home-based business and began selling her custom-made dog ID tags through her easy-to-navigate web site. Each tag is designed to last for years; they're handcrafted in nickel silver, which is corrosion-resistant and will not tarnish.

The handmade dog ID tags created by artist Sally Harrell are one-of-a-kind pieces of art that are practical, functional, and beautiful.

Harrell's circular tags are available in two sizes: ¾-inch and 1-inch diameter. The front prominently displays your dog's name, which is hand-engraved using one of several artistic fonts. The back is engraved with your name, phone number(s) and/or address. The back of the tag fits four lines of text, with up to twelve characters on each line.

Because each tag is custom made, the process takes about three weeks. Orders for these elegant ID tags can be placed online. They're ideal for male or female dogs of any size.

Gucci Heart and Dog Bone Pendant

Price: $90
Manufacturer: Gucci
Phone: (310) 278-3451 (Beverly Hills) or (212) 826-2600 (New York)
Web site: www.gucci.com
Availability: Online or from Gucci stores worldwide

This red enamel-and-nickel-plated brass pendant can be worn around your own neck as jewelry, or engraved and used on your dog's collar as her identification tag. Its lovely heart-shaped design has a red dog bone across the center of the pendant. Below the dog bone, the Gucci logo is engraved on the front. It's a little large, so this makes a perfect ID tag for medium and large dogs.

For small dogs, Gucci offers a red leather collar with a gold heart-shaped locket that can be engraved. The collar-pendant combination is $165.

To give your dog's collar a bit of extra bling, Gucci offers its famous interlocking G logo on a dog pendant that can be clipped onto any collar. The $105 pendant is available in brass or nickel-plated brass.

The Pet's Jeweler Diamond and Gold Dog Tags

Price: $700 to $2,400, and up
Manufacturer: The Pet's Jeweler
Web site: www.thepetsjeweler.com
Availability: Online

If diamonds are a girl's best friend and dogs are man's best friend, does that mean dogs love diamonds? Even if it's just you who likes the finer things in life, The Pet's Jeweler makes a selection of solid white or yellow 14-karat gold dog tags that are framed with hand-set diamonds. Talk about bling!

These handmade tags are rectangular and come in a variety of sizes. Each is custom-made and engraved with your dog's personal information. They offer the ultimate in elegance for your pampered pooch, or can be worn around your own neck as jewelry.

Who Can Resist?

When outside, virtually all dogs are attracted to fire hydrants and feel they must leave their mark whenever they encounter one. If you want your dog to have her own fire hydrant in your yard, check out Yuckos (314-770-1500; www.yuckos.com). You can order a replica fire hydrant ($150 to $375) made from bright red polyurethane (very washable!). The hydrants are 30 inches tall and come in a variety of styles.

For dog owners who simply want a solid-gold dog tag without the glitz of diamonds, several styles are available that are suitable for male or female dogs. Matching gold chain collars (these are decorative chains, not choke collars) are also available, starting at $200.

Bark Avenue Jewelers' Dog Tags and Pendants

Price: $250 to $2,500
Manufacturer: Bark Avenue Jewelers
Phone: (888) 268-1138
Web site: www.BarkAvenueJewelers.com
Availability: Online

Bark Avenue Jewelers will customize any existing dog tag, dog license, or rabies vaccination tag by surrounding it with a diamond or platinum frame and then accenting it with diamonds or other fine jewels.

While in New York, if you happen to make a wrong turn off Park Avenue, perhaps you'll find yourself on Bark Avenue, where all the really wealthy dogs shop for their fine jewelry. Inspired by New York's fine jewelers, Bark Avenue Jewelers offers a selection of handmade dog tags, made from 18-karat gold, platinum, and diamonds.

The company's Custom Designed Diamond Tag Jacket is priced around $2,500. It combines a rectangular tag in 18-karat gold and platinum, with a classic Elizabethan style, which is contradicted with a frame of smooth, bezel-set diamonds that will not catch on fur. For those of you who are counting, the diamonds are 2.5 carats total weight, G-H in color, and SI-2 in clarity.

The company also has a selection of collar pendants in popular shapes (such as a bone, paw, star, heart, and fire hydrant), also made from precious metals and fine stones. Many of these pendants are custom-made with your dog's name. The pendants start at $250 and go up considerably in price, based on the design and materials used.

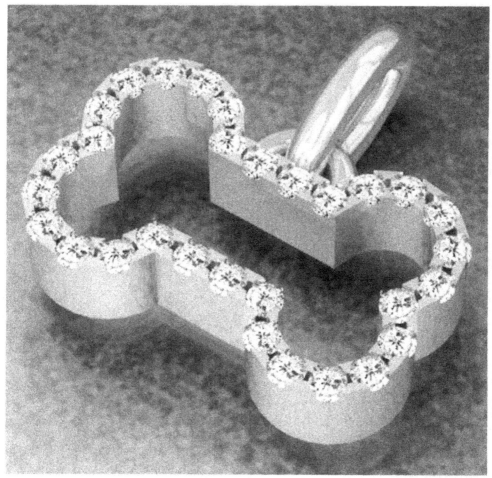

In addition to its line of ready-made tags, Bark Avenue Jewelers custom-designs gold, platinum, and diamond dog tags that are handmade works of art.

New Age Bling

Many people believe in the healing power of crystals and that these stones enable their wearer to take advantage of the special energies they give off. While people have tapped the power of crystals for millennia, now you can offer your dog a chance to accessorize her collar with crystal pendants, while potentially benefiting from the powers and metaphysical energies of these stones.

Several small companies, including Animal Amulets (805-967-0406; www.animalamulets.com), Charmed by Alecia (970-927-5290; www.charmedbyalecia.com), and Healing Pet Stones (888-398-7458; www.stone-healing.com), have handmade collar charms and accessories for your dog that have healing crystals. Designs can be customized to meet your dog's specific needs. These pendants and amulets clip onto any collar. Pet birthstone jewelry serves well as a great gift for animal lovers.

According to the Animal Amulets web site, "Gems and crystals are powerful conductors of universal energy. Their components are part earth and part star. The unique properties of each, built into their molecular code, bring forth different qualities and vibrations. When attuned to and worn, these frequencies can not only enhance beauty but promote health and positive change. The animulets are individually handcrafted by a small group of women artists with the finest materials available. The intuitive sequencing of the gems creates an energy pattern that gives each piece a life of its own."

Bella Tocca Dog Tags

Price: $48 to $60
Manufacturer: Bella Tocca Tags
Phone: (530) 292-3011
Web site: www.bellatoccatags.com
Availability: Online

Kate Dwyer, founder of Bella Tocca Tags, used to make jewelry for people. After her goldsmith's training in Europe, she went on to design, manufacture, and restore fine jewelry on both American coasts for twenty-five years. Only recently has she begun designing handmade dog tags that are truly works of art.

The original Bella Tocca Tag has a hand-pressed geometric design in German crystal, accented by a tiny turquoise at the base of the tag. It measures ⅞ inch high by 1 inch across and comes in a variety of color schemes, based on the semi-precious stones that serve as the centerpiece for each tag.

Bella Tocca Tags come in more than twenty unique and beautiful designs, offering everything from a simplistic look to more detailed and extravagant designs with various types of crystals used as accents. Your dog's name is engraved on the front of each tag. Your surname and phone number(s) are engraved on the back.

These beautiful tags are each custom-made and can only be ordered from the Bella Tocca Tags web site, which shows each of the tag designs and customization options in vivid color.

"Return to Tiffany" Tag and Tiffany Round Tag

Price: $400
Manufacturer: Tiffany & Co.
Phone: (800) 843-3269
Web site: www.tiffany.com
Availability: Online or from Tiffany & Co. jewelry stores or by mail order

Tiffany & Co. is one of the world's most well-known jewelers, offering a wide range of lovely products and wearable masterpieces. Featuring the "Return to Tiffany & Co. New York" slogan and logo, the company offers a solid 18-karat gold, heart-shaped dog tag, which can be custom engraved on the back. It's suitable to wear around your own neck as fine jewelry but will also look fabulous on your pampered pooch.

The company also makes a solid gold, circular dog tag that is blank on both sides but can be custom engraved. Of course, both products are delivered in Tiffany & Co.'s classic robin's egg blue gift box.

5

Dog Beds

Let Your Dog Lounge in Luxury

*M*ost dogs enjoy cuddling up next to their owners in bed and lounging on the living room couch. But not all dog owners allow this. If your dog needs his own place to lounge around and sleep but his taste in designer furniture is as discriminating as yours, you'll want to provide him with the most luxurious, comfortable, fashionable, and well-constructed bed available. After all, you want your dog to feel safe and comfortable when he's sleeping, don't you?

As you're about to discover, dog beds literally come in all shapes and sizes, plus they're constructed from a wide range of materials. Some dog beds are little more than oversized pillows that sit on the floor, while others are hand-crafted pieces of furniture designed to fit the décor of even the most prestigious home.

The two things to remember when selecting a dog bed for your pooch are:

1. No two dogs are alike. All dogs have their own personal preferences in terms of the style of bed they'll appreciate and find most comfortable. These preferences will most likely change at different stages of your dog's life.

2. Just because a particular bed *looks* comfortable and safe doesn't necessarily mean it is. Just as you'd shop around for the best and most comfortable bed for yourself, you'll probably want to do the same for your pooch.

This chapter focuses on a few of the many types of beds available, from overstuffed pillows to elaborate wood frame beds, complete with luxury mattresses. Keep in mind that the majority of these beds are designed for indoor use.

Choosing a Bed That's Right for Your Pooch

All indoor dogs should have a space at home to call their own. For the pampered pooch, this typically means having his own furniture. A designer bed that provides the ultimate in luxury, comfort, and security will do nicely.

To make sure you choose the perfect bed, consider the following points when making your decision:

+ Your dog's size

+ Your dog's age

+ Your dog's habits

+ Your dog's special needs

+ What the bed is made of

+ How easy the bed is to clean

+ Where the bed will be placed in your home and the available space

+ Your home décor

Puppies, for example, tend to prefer ultra-soft beds that are enclosed, at least around three sides. This creates a somewhat confined space, offering a greater sense of security. Older dogs might prefer a bed that's more open with a mattress that provides better support, especially if they have arthritis or other ailments.

The bed should be big enough for the dog to curl up or stretch out in comfort, without the risk of falling off or having part of his body hang off when he's asleep.

As you're looking for the ideal bed, consider the quality of construction and the materials the bed is made of, especially if your dog has a chewing habit. Some less expensive or poorly designed beds often have buttons, zipper pulls, exposed seams, or decorative accessories that can easily be chewed off and become a choking hazard. Others have low-quality upholstery that can easily be ripped.

Some beds are stuffed with chemically treated fill that gives off potentially toxic fumes which your dog will inhale while he sleeps. Others contain materials that could be a choking hazard if the dog rips open the pad or mattress. Always examine the bed's construction carefully. Ask yourself:

+ Is the bed well-constructed? Will it last for years?

+ Are the seams tightly sewn?

+ Is high-quality fabric used?

- Does the bed give off any chemical smell?

- Would the bed be ruined or permanently stained if the dog had an accident on or near it?

- Is the bed easily cleaned?

- Is the outer upholstery machine washable?

- Will the bed's materials retain and give off odors between cleanings?

- Is the size of the bed suitable for your dog? If your dog is still a growing puppy, does the bed provide room to grow?

Later, when the bed is in your home and being used, every month or so look at it again to make sure it's holding up.

The perfectly designed dog bed takes into consideration ease of cleaning, whether it's to control the natural odors that result from routine use or the accidents that are a normal part of every dog's life. Pillows and mattresses should be enclosed within a washable, water-resistant lining to protect the inner stuffing (whether that stuffing is cotton, foam, or polyester fill, all of which will retain odors without proper lining and protection).

You'll probably want the bed to fit in with your home's décor. Owners of truly pampered pooches can select a dog bed with a custom-designed mattress, frame, and/or pillow cover that coordinates perfectly with their curtains or the upholstery on the family sofa.

While the appearance of the dog bed may be important to you, your first and foremost consideration should be the health, comfort, and well-being of your dog. When it comes to providing your dog with the best that money can buy, you'll find a wide range of dog beds that are as elaborate, extravagant, and comfortable as any bed constructed for humans.

Step Up to Comfort

For dog owners who prefer to invite their pampered pooch into their own bed, C & D Pet Products (888-554-7387; www.cdpets.com) offers Pet Steps, designed to give smaller dogs easy access to people-size beds. With these solid wood steps next to your bed, your dog will be able to easily climb up and down without risking injury. The steps are available in five sizes, priced from $50 to $249, to accommodate the size of your pet and the height of your bed. They're also available in a wide range of colors. Within the housing of the steps are built-in drawers that provide handy storage space.

A less expensive step option is available from Doggy Steps ($39.99; www.doggysteps.com).

Sleep-N-Store Bed

Price: $500 and up
Manufacturer: Pets at Play
Phone: (877) 377-2789
Web site: www.petsatplay.com
Availability: Online or from upscale pet supply boutiques nationwide

Offering your dog the best of the best is rarely cheap. The Sleep-N-Store bed, for example, is priced starting at $500, but what you'll receive is perhaps the best designed, best constructed, and most comfortable bed available. In fact, it's so well-designed and such a stand-out that its inventor, Nancy Kerrigan (not the Olympic figure skater), holds several patents. The bed, along with Kerrigan, has been featured on numerous national television shows.

The Sleep-N-Store bed has a sturdy, handmade, solid wood frame and a memory foam mattress. Both the wood finish and the upholstery can be customized to complement your home's décor.

The Sleep-N-Store bed is functional yet looks like a fine piece of furniture. It comes in three sizes and is hand crafted in America. The bed's frame is made from solid ash. It has a built-in drawer, which can be used for organizing and storing your dog's toys or clothing.

The Sleep-N-Store bed's mattress is made from memory foam that is covered in a waterproof lining and upholstered in fine fabric. The wood finish and the upholstery come in a wide range of colors or can be custom ordered to match your home's décor.

"With its memory foam mattress, the bed was designed to provide the ultimate in comfort, but be extremely easy to clean," says Kerrigan, founder and president of Pets at Play. "The mattress cover and the bolster surrounding the edge of the mattress are machine washable and designed to last for many years.

"I designed the Sleep-N-Store bed for my own dog, Maggie, because when I was looking for a high-end bed that offered superior construction and that truly looked like a fine piece of furniture, I couldn't find one," Kerrigan continues. "Being a designer and inventor, I originally created the bed for use in my own home, but discovered that many other dog owners were looking for the same thing.

"Before I invented the Sleep-N-Store bed, the beds I found on the market that were considered high-end actually used very low-end fabric, for example, or offered poor-quality construction. They might have looked nice, but they didn't have that luxurious feel or they didn't fit into my home's décor at all," she adds.

Just like memory foam mattresses for humans, the one used with the Sleep-N-Store bed conforms perfectly to the body of your dog, based on the position he is lying in. It holds the dog's weight and takes the pressure off his muscles and bones. When he gets up from the bed, the memory foam returns to its original shape. It never requires any fluffing or shaking, unlike mattresses or pillows made from polyester fill or cotton, for example. For the dog's safety, the removable mattress is tied to the back of the bed so it won't slide when the dog jumps on or off.

"Throughout the entire design and manufacturing process for the Sleep-N-Store bed, I demanded the best of everything in terms of craftsmanship and materials, because that's what I wanted for my own dog," Kerrigan concludes. "When someone buys the Sleep-N-Store bed, I can proudly and confidently say they're getting exactly what they paid for."

Extra Luxury for Any Dog Bed

As an added luxury and to complement the memory foam mattress of the Sleep-N-Store bed, inventor Nancy Kerrigan has introduced a line of optional high-end goose down–filled pillows, blankets, and bedding. See the Pets at Play web site (www.petsatplay.com) for details about this ultra-soft, extremely warm line of bedding that's suitable for almost any dog bed.

Wouf Poof Leather Bone Bed

Price: $259
Manufacturer: Wouf Poof
Phone: (888) 828-9764
Web site: www.woufpoof.com
Availability: Online or from upscale pet supply boutiques nationwide

Some of the finest furniture in our homes is covered in leather. So why not invest in high-end leather furniture for your dog? The Wouf Poof Leather Bone bed is shaped like a dog bone and is made from ultra-soft leather. Designed for dogs who weigh under 15 pounds, it offers a flat, pillowlike style with a slight indentation in the center for the dog to snuggle in. The bed is approximately 5 inches thick and measures 25 by 20 inches. For medium dogs (15 to 35 pounds), the company offers a larger paw-shaped leather bed.

Made from ultra-soft leather, the Wouf Poof Bone bed is for dogs under 15 pounds and comes in a variety of colors. It's easy to clean and coordinates nicely with the décor in most homes.

Available in an assortment of colors, the bed is designed to provide comfort, durability, and safety. The nontoxic leather does not absorb odors, nor does it promote bacterial growth, the way many fabrics do. It's easy to clean using a damp cloth.

Louisdog Blue House

Price: $105 and up
Manufacturer: Louisdog
Phone: (011) 82-2-541-1640
Web site: www.louisdog.com
Availability: Upscale pet supply boutiques worldwide

Based in Seoul, South Korea, Louisdog is a premier brand of upscale dog products that is quickly gaining fame throughout the world. The company has distribution throughout Europe, Asia, and North America and makes a wide range of high-quality dog furniture, clothing, toys, and accessories. Many of the products are designed using pastel colors, such as baby blue, pink, yellow, and green, and most are nicely color coordinated.

The Louisdog Blue House, for example, is an ultra-plush bed that's enclosed around three sides to provide a dog with comfort and security. This particular bed will appeal to puppies, thanks to its criblike design. On either side of the bed are handles, which make it easy to carry (although the bed

The Blue House is just one example of Louisdog's plush beds. The "Kashwere" blanket here is described on page 71.

is extremely lightweight), plus the bottom is lined with waterproof material to contain accidents. The bed is machine washable and easy to maintain.

Available in two sizes, this bed is constructed using durable denim on the outside and 100 percent gingham-patterned cotton on the inside. It's just one of more than a dozen dog bed designs offered by Louisdog.

Crypton Dog Bed

Price: $190 to $300 and up
Manufacturer: Hi Tex, Inc., Crypton Super Fabrics
Phone: (800) CRYPTON
Web site: www.cryptonfabric.com
Availability: Online

If your dog has managed to chew, scratch, or stain his previous dog bed to the point where it's beyond repair, the Crypton Dog Bed is your answer. These beds, available in rectangular, round, or donut shapes, in multiple sizes and a wide range of colors, are constructed using the patented Crypton Super Fabric.

The Crypton Dog Bed has a plush, pillowlike design and is made from the patented Crypton Super Fabric, which resists stains, moisture, odor, and bacteria.

According to the company, Crypton Super Fabric is an engineered textile that is stain, water, and bacteria resistant. "The key to this super fabric is its [patented] weaving process, coupled with its proven barrier; nothing gets through Crypton to the cushion . . . nothing." Currently, Crypton fabric is being used in a wide range of products, including linens and décor in hotels and aboard cruise ships. But because it's so easy to clean, durable, and extremely soft, it's also the perfect upholstery for a dog bed.

Since the fabric is available in so many colors and patterns (including a suede-like finish), and the dog beds themselves are offered in a variety of different shapes and sizes, the manufacturer has created a unique Design Your Own Dog Bed service on its web site. The bed can even be monogrammed at no additional charge.

From the Crypton Super Fabrics Design Your Own Dog Bed Web site (www.cryptonfabric.com), first choose the shape of the bed, then the size (based on the size of your dog). Using on-screen fabric swatches, select the top, middle, and bottom fabric colors. Of course, you can choose the same color, or add a two-tone or three-tone look to the bed. Finally, select the monogram you'd like sewn into the bed and the thread color. You'll then see an on-screen preview of what your bed will look like. Upon placing your order, the bed will be manufactured and shipped directly to your home.

Every Shape Imaginable

Snooty Pets (www.snootypets.com) offers a lovely handmade sleigh bed with curved, sweeping arms, rich mahogany stain, and cushions fit for aristocracy ($320.99). It measures 29 by 28 by 17 inches. The mattress and linens come in three designs and patterns.

Meanwhile, Lucky Dog (www.shopluckydog.com) sells a dog bed shaped like a sports car that's designed by Haute Diggity Dog. The Furcedes Sports Car Bed is priced at $259. Other designs include beds shaped like a New York City taxi and the Barkswaggin' Bed.

Crypton **Dog Beds** are well-constructed, durable, and soft. The upper upholstery is easily removable for cleaning and uses a strong Velcro closure instead of a zipper. These are plush, pillow-shaped beds that can be placed on a floor or within a dog house.

Other Options for the Discriminating Dog

What, you haven't found the perfect dog bed yet? There are still plenty of options that offer unique designs and special functionality. The following is information about a handful of additional premium quality dog beds you won't find at your typical pet supply store.

Fatboy Doggielounge

Price: $99 and $139
Manufacturer: Fatboy USA
Phone: (919) 942-1608
Web site: www.fatboyusa.com
Availability: Dealers worldwide

The Fatboy Doggielounge can best be described as a rectangular beanbag for your dog. It was created in Finland by award-winning designer Jukka Setala and provides a plush, pillow-like sleeping area. The bed is available in seven colors and two sizes (24 by 32 inches and 32 by 48 inches). It's made from a soft nylon material and has a PVC coating, making it stain and water resistant. The outer bag (the upholstery) is machine washable.

Petsafe Wellness Bed

Price: $75 to $120
Manufacturer: Radio Systems Corp.
Phone: (800) 732-2677
Web site: www.petsafe.net
Availability: Online and from upscale pet supply boutiques nationwide

This bed is constructed using a 3-inch-thick orthopedic foam core and has a soft, cream-colored, washable fleece cover. A special plug-in unit provides heat and a vibrating massage. The built-in timer

---

A Blanket for Your Baby

In many ways dogs, especially puppies, are like human babies. They have their favorite toys and most love cuddling up in an ultra-soft blanket. Mellow Mutts offers a lovely, chocolate brown "Kashwere" blanket that features a stitched dog paw design in the corner ($105; 866-475-MUTT; www.mellowmutts.com). This 30- by 30-inch blanket is machine washable and is perfect for puppies and small dogs. It can be placed in a dog bed or a carrier. (You can see photos of this ultra-soft blanket on pages 69 and 82.)

You'll also find a collection of Nature Nap fleece dog beds priced under $50 at the Only Natural Pet Store web site (888-937-6677; www.onlynaturalpet.com).

means you can set how long the heat and/or massage operates. Older dogs, in particular, will enjoy the message, warmth, and support this bed offers. It should not, however, be used with a dog who tends to chew cables, since this bed has a four-foot electric cord attached to it. The bed comes in several sizes.

Gel-Pedic Pet Bed

Price: $95 to $200
Manufacturer: Splintek
Phone: (888) PET-PADS
Web site: www.gelpedic.com
Availability: Online

These oval beds enable a dog to cuddle up in a natural, nesting position as he sinks into the GelFoam that molds to his body and eases the pressure on his bones and muscles. The 3½-inch thick GelFoam is designed to keep the dog cool in the summer and warm in the winter. The bed is available in five sizes to accommodate everyone from a toy dog to an 80-pound pooch. The outer cover upholstery is machine washable and comes in a variety of colors. An optional "leak liner" is also available. One unique feature of this dog bed is that it uses a proprietary Repel-a-Flea system—two to four packets of natural ground eucalyptus, placed in special reservoir pouches that are molded into the GelFoam bed. The natural eucalyptus will repel fleas, mites, and ticks, plus help control odors.

Pluscious Pet Décor

Price: $500 to $1,000 and up
Manufacturer: Pluscious
Phone: (877) 738-3326
Web site: www.pluscious.com
Availability: Online and from upscale pet supply boutiques and department stores (including Harrod's in London)

If you're looking for a dog bed inspired by a luxurious designer bed for humans, plus one that offers a hand-crafted wooden frame accessorized with a plush mattress and lovely linens, check out the fine furniture created and built by Pluscious's founders, Paul Mankelow and Andre Ricard. Offering more than nine luxurious designs, each accessorized with fine fabric upholstery and linens, these beds will look great in any home. Each bed design can be fully customized when ordered. They're stunningly beautiful and truly the ultimate choice for any pampered pooch.

Pet Tent

Price: $175 to $200
Manufacturer: The Persnickety Pet
Phone: (402) 556-3323
Web site: www.pettents.com
Availability: Online and from upscale pet supply boutiques

Providing your small dog with an enclosed, tentlike bed offers him security, comfort, and privacy as he sleeps and relaxes. The Persnickety Pet's luxury beds, called Pet Tents, are made from top-quality materials and are designed to enhance any décor. The company makes about ten enclosed tentlike designs that will make your pooch feel like royalty. Each tent houses one of the company's signature sleeping cushions, filled with buckwheat hulls. Both the external tent and the cushion cover are washable. Pet Tents require minimal assembly.

Pet Tents come in a variety of styles and include an enclosed area for your dog to sleep. Each tent comes with a sleeping cushion filled with natural buckwheat hulls.

6

Toys and Activities

Entertaining Your Dog

Most dogs love interacting with people and other dogs, plus they absolutely love to play. While the latest Xbox 360 or PlayStation 2 video games might be on the top of your child's list of ways to have fun, your dog has more simple desires. This chapter features some of the many ways you can entertain your dog, and some of the more educational toys that are available for her.

Most people who want to pamper their dog will leave out an abundance of toys to play with, but most trainers and animal behavior experts agree that it's best to give your dog just two or three toys at a time. Rotate them periodically to keep the dog interested. Dogs, like kids, can be finicky when it comes to their toys. One day she might play with a toy for hours, while the next day it sits under a chair, ignored. However, if your dog makes it clear she has a favorite toy, leave that one out where she can always get it.

Some other things to remember about dog toys:

✦ Some dog toys are not suitable for some dogs. Choose toys that are appropriate for your dog's size, personality, chewing habits, and energy level.

✦ When giving your dog any new toy to play with, supervise her for the first few play sessions. Make sure she's playing with it properly and safely.

✦ It's important to keep your dog's toys clean. Clean them every week or two, or after the toy has been played with outside or just looks dirty. Don't use any chemicals or hazardous cleaning products. If possible, follow the cleaning directions provided with the toy.

And the most important thing to remember: Giving your dog lots of toys is *not* a replacement for spending quality time with her and giving her the love and attention she wants and needs.

Fetch 101

What could be more fun for your dog than spending time outside with you, playing the age-old game of fetch or having you throw a soft ball (or a plush toy) around the living room while you're watching television?

Fetch is a simple game that most dogs love. It's interactive, allows dogs to burn off excess energy, and it can provide unlimited fun. It's an activity most dogs never get bored with, plus it's a wonderful bonding activity for you and your pampered pooch. With a bit of training, you'll be able to throw an object and have your dog chase after it, return to you, drop it in your hand or at your feet, and get excited for another fun-filled round.

You can buy all sorts of fancy balls, flying discs, and other toys to play fetch with, but most dogs will be quite content playing with an ordinary stick.

Pampering your pooch with a game of fetch doesn't require any fancy equipment. In fact, depending on the size of your dog, a rubber ball, flying disc (Frisbee), or even a stick you pick up outside is all you need to start playing.

GoDogGo Ball Launcher
Price: $149.95
Manufacturer: GoDogGo
Web site: www.buygodoggo.com
Availability: Online

For dog owners who can't throw a ball far enough or often enough to make a game of fetch fun for their dog, GoDogGo has a solution for medium to large dogs. This is an automated game of fetch that includes a remote-controlled ball launcher. The GoDogGo launcher will throw up to fifteen tennis balls, one at a time, that your dog can chase after, catch, and return without you ever having to lift a finger (except to hit a button on the unit's remote control).

There are several game play modes, so you can set the system to launch tennis balls on your command, or do it automatically every seven or fifteen seconds. When the launcher is empty, you simply refill the bucket with balls, and your dog will be ready for plenty of additional fun. Each ball will be launched between 15 and 30 feet.

The GoDogGo system runs on batteries or can be plugged into an electrical outlet. It weighs 11 pounds, so it can be taken anywhere there's space for your dog to run around and play. Of course, this device is for outdoor use only.

Life Is Good Flying Disc

Price: $12 and $16
Manufacturer: Life Is Good
Phone: (888) 878-2987
Web site: www.lifeisgood.com
Availability: Online and from Life Is Good stores nationwide

The Life Is Good flying disc is a great toy for playing fetch outdoors.

The flying disc from Life Is Good comes in 6-inch and 9-inch diameters. It's made of a durable, light-blue, ballistic nylon material (exceptionally strong fabric used by soft luggage manufacturers, for example, that resists tearing or punctures) and has a reflective silver and orange edge. After playtime, the disc can also be used as a portable water bowl. The disc is well balanced to ensure maximum distance with every throw. Embroidered with the Life Is Good dog icon, this is a great toy for playing fetch. A matching collar, leash, bowl, and ball are also available.

Launch-A-Ball

Price: $7.99
Manufacturer: The Kyjen Company
Phone: (800) 477-5735
Web site: www.kyjen.com/dogtoys
Availability: Pet supply stores and upscale pet supply boutiques nationwide

Most people get tired of playing fetch long before their dog does. Launch-A-Ball is a plastic handle that can be used to scoop up tennis balls or other small balls from the ground (so you don't have to keep bending down). You can also use the handle to launch balls into the air with a lot less effort than you'd need just using your arm. (Think lacrosse.) You can also throw the ball a lot farther, which means your dog gets more exercise. If your dog loves playing fetch, Launch-A-Ball is a cool game play accessory for people. It's designed for outdoor use.

Chew Toys

Dogs love chewing. It relieves stress and boredom, exercises their jaws and teeth, and fulfills some very basic canine need. In fact, given the opportunity, most will chew on just about anything. Keeping your dog from chewing on furniture or other items you'd just as soon keep out of her mouth will require some training on your part. You also need to provide her with a few chew toys she can munch on. Dogs can be a bit finicky, but once you find a chew toy she loves, she'll probably spend countless hours jawing it.

Chew toys are divided into two categories: edible and nonedible. Edible chew toys are bones and other treats that can be eaten and easily digested by your dog. See chapter 2 for examples of healthy and edible hard chews. Nonedible chew toys can be made of a variety of materials, including rubber, plastic, cloth, and rope. This section describes a handful of popular chew toys you'll find at your local pet supply store.

When you go shopping for chew toys, keep in mind the following:

✦ It's important to give your dog chew toys specifically designed for dogs. A child's plush teddy bear, for example, often has plastic eyes or outfits with buttons that can be ripped off and cause choking.

✦ When giving your dog any chew toy, make sure it's totally safe. It should contain no parts that can be torn apart and become a choking hazard.

✦ No matter what type of chew toy you give your dog, examine it periodically to make sure it hasn't become worn out or overchewed. With a rope toy, for example, if you see the material starting to shred or the knots on either end becoming loose or torn apart, replace the toy.

✦ Keep in mind that no dog toy is totally indestructible. It's the nature of chews toys that they will have to periodically be replaced. Be sure to replace nonedible chew toys when the products get worn down, or if they become too small for your dog to chew safely.

Rope Toy
Price: $8.95 to $12.95
Manufacturer: EcoAnimal
Phone: (702) 543-7003

Web site: www.ecoanimal.com/dog_toys.html
Availability: Pet supply stores and upscale pet supply boutiques nationwide

Tip Many dog owners set aside a toy chest for their pampered pooch, using a basket with a lid, or a large plastic storage container.

Rope toys have become very popular chew toys for dogs. The toy is simply a thick piece of rope with tight knots on both ends. Most rope toys are made from a cotton yarn that is easily washable. They come in a variety of sizes. A rope toy will help keep your dog's teeth and gums healthy, while entertaining her and helping her satisfy her need to chew or teethe.

EcoAnimal has taken the basic rope toy design and manufactured a version using all-natural hemp. These toys are ideal for heavy chewers and come in two sizes: 9 ⅔ inches and 14 inches long.

Kong

Price: $6 to $20
Manufacturer: The Kong Company
Phone: (303) 216-2626
Web site: www.kongcompany.com
Availability: Pet supply stores nationwide

The Kong Company released the first rubber Kong toy in 1976 and changed the chew toy market forever. The original Kong toy is made from a bright red, super-bouncy rubber. It's hollow inside, which means it can be stuffed with your dog's favorite biscuits, peanut butter, or specially made Kong Stuff'N products (sold separately, see chapter 2), to provide even more enjoyment.

Kongs come in several sizes and consistencies. Choose one for your dog based on her size and chewing habits. Because they are made from durable rubber and come in bright colors and unique designs (made to promote chewing, bounding, rolling, and other behaviors), Kongs have become widely used for therapy and to prevent boredom, separation anxiety, and other behavioral issues. When used in conjunction with treats, these toys become even more irresistible. Regular use of Kongs can also improve oral health, according to the company.

The Kong Company sells a variety of different chewing toys in addition to the classic Kong. The Kong Flyer, for example, is a flying disc that's made of the same chewable material as the classic Kong toys. The Kong Dental Stick is a hollow, round rubber toy with grooves on the outside (to promote your dog's dental health and oral hygiene), and treats or peanut butter can be stuffed inside. Kong Retriever toys are classic Kongs with durable rope attached to them that can be used for tugging. The ultrabouncy Kong Jump'N Jack is an alternative to a ball. It's shaped like a large toy jack, but it's made from the same rubber as the classic Kong.

The Kong is one of the most popular chew toys on the market. The unusual design provides a wide range of interaction possibilities for your dog.

Kong Time

Price: $139.99
Manufacturer: Dogopolis
Phone: (800) 995-8996
Web site: www.kongtime.com
Availability: Online and pet supply stores nationwide

Once your dog is hooked on Kongs, the Kong Time dispenser is great for people who work full time and must leave their dog alone all day. You can load up to four Kongs (prestuffed with treats) into the dispenser, which then releases them, one-at-a-time, at random intervals (for up to eight hours). The

Kong Time dispenser is battery-operated and comes with four Kongs, plus an assortment of sample treats. It's a great way to keep your dog entertained throughout the day. It's truly a home entertainment system for dogs.

One caveat: Kong Time is designed for households with only one dog (unless the dogs are kept separated when they're home alone). You don't want fights to break out over who gets the Kong.

Nylabone

Price: $3.99 and up
Manufacturer: Nylabone Products
Phone: (800) 631-2188
Web site: www.nylabone.com
Availability: Pet supply stores nationwide

Nylabone makes a line of extremely popular, nonedible chew toys made from a soft thermoplastic polymer with a shape that's easy for your dog to hold and chew. These toys are flavored, which makes them practically irresistible. Dogs have been known to spend up to several hours each day enjoying these chew toys.

Nylabone nonedible chew toys (the company also makes a line of edible chews and treats) come in a variety of sizes and flavors. Choose a size that's suitable for your dog. Some dogs may have a particular preference in terms of flavor, but all are designed to be extremely appealing to your pampered pooch. Nylabone's products are designed to promote good dental hygiene, enhance overall mental fitness, and encourage positive behavior, according to the company.

Although they're nontoxic, Nylabone nonedible chew toys are not intended to be swallowed. The toy has tiny bristlelike raised projections that help clean a dog's teeth. The company reports that during normal chewing, these tiny pieces (which are no larger than a grain of rice) are sometimes ingested. They should just pass through the dog. However, the dog should not be able to break off large pieces of any Nylabone nonedible chew toy. It's important to inspect your dog's Nylabone often to make sure it's intact, with no large missing pieces.

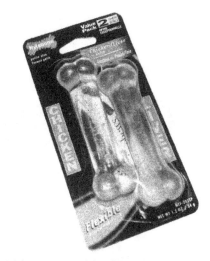

Nylabone nonedible chew toys come in a variety of flavors and sizes. Most dogs absolutely love them.

Plush and Squeaky Toys

Just like human toddlers, puppies and even adult dogs often become emotionally attached to a favorite plush toy. They'll carry it around on walks, cuddle up with it at night, feel safer when they travel with it, and play with it throughout the day. Plush toys for dogs come in all shapes and sizes. When choosing one for your dog, make sure it's well made, has no small pieces that can be torn off and become a choking hazard, and that it's totally nontoxic and easily washable. Plush toys for dogs often have a built-in squeaker, so when your dog bites into it, it makes a quick, high-pitched noise she loves. Of course, if the dog ever tears the toy apart, that squeaker can also become a choking hazard, so periodically inspect your dog's plush toys for tears.

Louisdog's Cookie Boy is an adorable, human-shaped plush toy for dogs. It's about 6 inches tall and has a built-in squeaker that puppies, in particular, will love.

Most dogs are somewhat particular about the plush toys they play with, but once they choose a favorite, they become inseparable from it.

Many companies sell quality plush toys for dogs. You'll find them at your favorite pet supply store. In addition, the American Kennel Club (www.akc.org) has a full line of adorable and safe plush toys for dogs. (Your dog need not be purebred to play!) Louisdog (www.louisdog.com) also makes a selection of cute plush toys, including a toy shaped like a human that's made of terrycloth that puppies, in particular, will love. The Louisdog Cookie Boy comes in baby blue or orange, and is $11. The bone-shaped plush toy from Louisdog is also a favorite.

Toys That Make Your Dog Think

When you visit any pet supply store, you'll find dozens, perhaps hundreds of dog toys to choose from. How do you choose? The following toys are designed to make your dog think and improve her puzzle-solving skills, coordination, and attention span as she plays with them.

iCube and iCube II Cagey Cube

Price: $12.95
Manufacturer: The Kyjen Company/Plush Puppies
Phone: (800) 477-5735
Web site: www.kyjen.com/dogtoys
Availability: Pet supply stores and upscale pet supply boutiques nationwide

Made of a durable, plush material, the iCube is essentially a brightly colored, soft, hollow cube that contains a trap door on every side. You place brightly colored balls within the cube, and your dog must use her snout and paws to figure out how to remove the balls to play with them. It's a fun toy that can be used by your dog when she's alone, or something you can play with together. Combine it with a game of fetch as she removes the hidden balls.

The iCube II is based on the same concept, but instead of brightly colored plush balls, the toy uses several smaller plush toys of different shapes and colors. Both toys come in two sizes and are designed primarily for indoor use, although the cube and the balls are washable.

These two toys are ingeniously designed and will encourage your dog to think while having fun. Every ball or plush shape that goes inside the cube has a built-in squeaker.

The iCube (right) is a fun, durable, and well-designed toy that includes a puzzle-like element to make your dog think as she plays. With IntelliBone (left), dogs must figure out how to remove the plush, multicolored rings.

IntelliBone

Price: $14.95
Manufacturer: The Kyjen Company/Plush Puppies
Phone: (800) 477-5735
Web site: www.kyjen.com/dogtoys
Availability: Pet supply stores and upscale pet supply boutiques nationwide

The fun with IntelliBone begins when you take a series of five brightly colored, plush rings and place them around a long, plush bone-shaped object. Your dog must then figure out the best way to remove each ring from the bone, so each can be used as a squeaky chew toy. It's a simple concept, but it will likely entertain your dog for hours. Like the iCube, the IntelliBone is durable and washable, plus it provides a great way to eliminate boredom. It comes in two sizes.

Buster Cube

Price: $14.99 to $16.99
Manufacturer: The Kruuse Group
Web site: www.bustercube.com
Availability: Pet supply stores and upscale pet supply boutiques nationwide

This solid plastic cube is a fun, puzzlelike toy. You load the hollow center with your dog's favorite crunchy treats, and then, as she pushes the cube around on the floor, she must figure out how to release the treats from the small hole on the side of the cube. As she moves the cube, your dog will hear the treats rolling around inside, plus she'll be able to smell them.

As the dog gets more experienced and empties the cube faster, you can increase the level of difficulty by adjusting the speed at which the food is released during play. The Buster Cube can be loaded with any small and hard treat, or pieces of a biscuit. (Chapter 2 offers some healthy suggestions.)

The original Buster Cube is a durable, 4 ½-inch plastic cube that's available in bright red or blue. It's ideal for dogs over 22 pounds. The 3 ¼-inch Buster MiniCube is a smaller version.

Treats fall out of the side hole as your dog rolls and pushes the Buster Cube.

Ultimate Puppy Toolkit

Designed by veterinarians and animal behavior specialists, the Ultimate Puppy Toolkit is a collection of informational booklets written to help you raise and train your new puppy. It's comprised of six relatively short, easy-to-understand booklets that include photos, plus a poster and a handy pocket reference guide. This kit includes training tips and other information, and also contains detailed information on a wide range of educational games you can play with your dog, including activities that will exercise her brain as well as her body.

The kit comes in a cardboard box and is designed to help guide you through the first sixteen weeks of your puppy's life. Even if you're experienced at raising and training dogs, the innovative ideas in the thirty-three-page *Games* booklet, for example, will provide valuable information and ideas about how to entertain and occupy your dog. As you teach your dog these games, you'll be able to reinforce commands, such as "take it," "leave it," "drop it," "come," "stay," "follow," and "retrieve." The twenty-page *Socialize* booklet will help you train your dog to get along and play with other dogs and humans.

The Ultimate Puppy Toolkit is made by Urban Puppy (416-465-1992; www.urbanpuppy.com) and is available online and from pet supply stores nationwide.

Leo

Price: $18.95
Manufacturer: Canine Genius
Web site: www.caninegenius.com
Availability: Online and from upscale pet supply boutiques nationwide

Designed to be a cross between a Kong and a Buster Cube, Leo is a toy and puzzle combo that was named after human genius Leonardo DaVinci. It's shaped sort of like a bowling pin with a hollow center, and several can be connected together to make the toy more challenging. Because of its unique shape, the Leo is fun for bouncing, fetching, tugging, and as a challenging treat-dispensing toy for medium to soft chewers. There's also a version made for harder chewers. It comes in three colors and is suitable for medium to large dogs.

Agility Training

When your dog is trained and understands all of the basic commands, including "sit," "stay," "come," and "down," you can teach her basic agility exercises. Agility training is an interactive activity for you and your dog. It involves teaching your dog to navigate an obstacle course composed of tunnels, jumps, ramps, seesaws, ladders, and other challenges. Many professional dog training schools teach agility. There are also agility competitions held regularly around the country.

Agility is considered a canine sport, and competitors can earn titles from several organizations. During a competition, the dog's handler is given a set amount of time in which to direct the dog through an obstacle course, without using a leash. The first organized agility event was held in 1979, as part of the Crufts Dog Show in Britain. The sport is loosely modeled after equestrian stadium jumping competitions, but has evolved to include a variety of obstacles and activities.

To learn more about agility training and competitions, contact the United States Dog Agility Association (www.usdaa.com), the North American Dog Agility Council (www.nadac.com), or the American Kennel Club (www.akc.org).

To buy professional-quality dog agility training equipment, including jumps, seesaws, tunnels, and ladders, visit the Max 200 web site (www.max200.com), Weave Poles (www.weave-poles.com), Clean Run (www.cleanrun.com), and Affordable Agility (www.affordableagility.com). From these sites, you can also order high-end equipment, videos, books, and agility supplies.

Agility Starter Set Obstacle Course

Price: $39.99
Manufacturer: The Kyjen Company
Phone: (800) 477-5735
Web site: www.kyjen.com/dogtoys
Availability: Pet supply stores and upscale pet supply boutiques nationwide

The Dog Agility Starter Set Obstacle Course comes with the tools you'll need to set up a simple obstacle course, so you can teach your dog the very basics of agility in your own backyard. The set includes a number of agility obstacles, including a collapsible tunnel, weave poles, and a small jump. It's not a replacement for the professional equipment you'll find at an agility training school, but this set provides a fun outdoor activity for you to share with your dog.

The New Team Sport Sweeping America

If your dog is well trained and extremely active, consider getting her involved in another canine sport, fly ball. Fly ball is a team sport, and was invented in California in the late 1970s. Here's how it works: Fly ball races match two teams of four dogs each, racing side by side, over a 51-foot-long course. Each dog must run in relay fashion down a row of jumps, trigger a lever on a fly ball box, which tosses a ball into the air, catch the ball, and return over the jumps. The next dog is then released to run the course, but can't cross the start/finish line until the previous dog has returned over all four jumps and reached the start/finish line. The first team to have all four dogs complete the course without error wins the heat. The height of the jumps is determined by the smallest dog on each team.

North American Flyball Association (NAFA) tournaments are divided into divisions, so teams compete against other teams of equal abilities. All dogs, including mixed breeds, are eligible to compete and earn titles in NAFA-sanctioned tournaments.

Legend has it that Herbert Wagner ran the first fly ball race on *The Tonight Show with Johnny Carson*. Soon afterward, dog trainers and clubs were making and using fly ball boxes. In the early 1980s the sport became so popular that NAFA was formed. This is the worldwide authority for fly ball. Since the early 1980s, organized fly ball teams have formed throughout the country and competitions and tournaments are held throughout the year. There are more than 700 registered fly ball clubs, with more than 16,000 members nationwide, according to NAFA.

To learn more about fly ball, visit the official NAFA web site (www.fly ball.org).

7

Accessories for Pets and People

Innovative Ways to Show Off Your Love

The bond between a dog and his owner is usually a special one. It's sometimes rather private, as well. But if you want to show the world how much you love your dog, there are plenty of ways to do it. You can decorate your home with custom-created, museum-quality photographs and artwork featuring your dog, or carry with you a piece of hand-crafted jewelry. You're about to discover just some of your options.

Custom Jewelry

Nothing says "I love you" like jewelry. In addition to jewelry for dogs, a variety of companies make jewelry for people that can be customized and enable you to show the world your love for your dog, even when your dog isn't around.

PawPrints Jewelry

Manufacturer: PawPrints Jewelry
Phone: (866) 729-7769
Web site: www.pawprintsjewelry.com
Availability: Online

Linda Roberts has a degree in Fine Arts from California State University, Hayward. In the past, her work has been commissioned by the Walt Disney Company and sold at the Smithsonian Museum Shop in Washington, D.C. Much of her professional life, however, has been in radio broadcasting.

That was, until her dog, Bear, was about to die. Using her artistic and jewelry-making skills, Roberts created a pure silver pendant for herself that incorporated the actual paw print of her beloved dog. It was a keepsake that helped keep her close to Bear after his death.

The one-of-a-kind jewelry she created for herself from a clay imprint of her dog's paw became a prototype for the work she now does with her company, PawPrints Jewelry. Today, Roberts sells her unique pieces to dog owners throughout the country. She has also expanded her product line to include pendants, key rings, tie tacks, cuff links, and other "companion keepsakes."

When you place an order for a PawPrints Jewelry pendant, you'll receive a Paw Impression Kit, which Roberts designed. In about ten minutes, you can create a clay imprint of your dog's paw using materials supplied within the kit. Once the clay hardens, return the imprint in a postage-paid box. Roberts then goes to work handcrafting a one-of-a-kind, pure silver pendant featuring the dog's print. Within three weeks, you receive a pendant that is suitable for men or women. The price starts at $200.

"My customers are people who care about their dog and who realize their dog isn't going to live forever," says Roberts. "The jewelry I create serves as a token of love while the dog is still alive and after he's gone.

"One way my business has evolved has been by handling special requests from customers. I have done a few projects for customers where I created a pure silver paw print pendant for the dog owner to wear, plus a collar pendant for a dog that featured an imprint of the owner's hand," she adds.

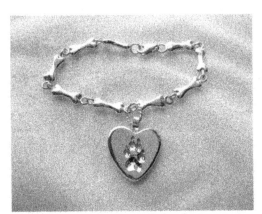

Created from a clay imprint of a dog's own paw, each of PawPrints Jewelry's pieces is unique.

PawPrints Jewelry pendants come in two sizes and in five different shapes, so each customer can have a truly personalized piece.

Roberts continues, "My jewelry is a celebration of the relationship between the dog and their owner. The concept of my jewelry is very adaptable. It's also very personal. I have created pendants out of gold and platinum, based on a customer's wishes. The most rewarding aspect of my work is the reaction I receive from my clients, who are touched so deeply when they receive their pendant. It's one thing to wear a pendant with a generic paw print that shows your love for dogs. It's another thing altogether to know that the paw print was created directly from an impression of your own dog's paw. It's this personalization and customization that makes my pendants something people can treasure for many years. I have heard so many heartwarming stories from my customers that somehow involve my pendants."

Roberts spends more than fifteen hours handcrafting each piece. "This isn't something created from a mass production line," she says. "I take a tremendous amount of pride in my work."

A PawPrints Jewelry pendant is a wonderful item to purchase for yourself, but they also make great gifts for anyone with a dog. The PawPrints Jewelry dog paw pendants come in ½-inch and 1-inch sizes and in five different shapes (diamond, heart, dog tag, oval, and circle). The paw can be created as an imprint or as a relief on the pendant, which is made from 0.999 pure silver. Each pendant comes in a lovely wooden jewelry box. A wide variety of matching chains are also available.

Pet Photography

Throughout your dog's life, one of the best ways to document major milestones and memorable moments is to take a photograph. When it comes to pet photography, you have three major options.

- ✦ You can take photos yourself.

- ✦ You can have relatively inexpensive photos taken at a local portrait studio, pet supply store, or some department stores. Be sure to call the portrait studio first to make an appointment and confirm that they're willing to photograph pets.

- ✦ You can commission a professional pet photographer to take fine art–quality portraits of your dog. This option is the most expensive, but the end result will be far superior.

Once you've had photographs or portraits taken of your dog that capture his appearance and personality, you can incorporate the photographs into an album or scrapbook, frame them for display in your home or office, or have a wide range of personalized items (such as coffee mugs, mouse pads, checks, and even postage stamps) created that incorporate your dog's image.

Jim Dratfield's Petography

Manufacturer: Jim Dratfield
Phone: (800) 738-6472
Web site: www.petography.com
Availability: By appointment

Many professional photographers around the country accept commissions to photograph pets. However, only a handful of highly skilled photographers have dedicated their careers exclusively to photographing animals. Jim Dratfield is one. His work has appeared in more than a hundred publications, including *InStyle, O, The Oprah Magazine, Elle Décor,* and *Town & Country,* plus in nine of his own photography books.

Taking the art of photographing animals to a new level of creativity—a process Dratfield calls Petography—since 1993 he has been commissioned to photograph thousands of pets all over the world.

He explains, "I believe that many things touch us throughout our lives, but it's often our pets who are there for us in both good times and bad. Petography provides people a way to remember those times and those pets forever."

He continues, "I have seen a lot of really bad pet photography that was not fine art quality and that was extremely impersonal. I wanted to offer something different. While I am based in New York, I travel across the country and throughout the world to take photographs. When I photograph an animal, I try to shoot at a location where that animal is the most comfortable or familiar, such as their home. This helps me to capture their personality. When I photograph someone's pet, I often encourage the pet's owner to be in the photographs so I can capture that relationship or bond on film."

Dratfield has been hired by dozens of celebrities, along with hundreds of everyday people who want to capture the true essence of their pet's appearance and personality in an artistic and one-of-a-kind portrait. The cost of a single photography session with Dratfield begins at $1,100 (plus airfare and travel expenses if you're not in New York) and takes up to four hours. After the photo session, it will take several weeks for the prints to be done.

"As an artist, I believe it's my eye that sets my work apart," says Dratfield. "It's something that's hard to quantify. When I begin photographing a dog, I never have a predetermined time limit or number of rolls of film to shoot. Every situation is totally different. I don't expect dogs to model. I work at their pace. I first need to build up the dog's trust. I might spend an hour or more with a dog before I ever snap a single photograph. I know every dog is an individual. That's what I am trying to show in my photographs."

Dratfield has worked with animal trainers to better understand animal behavior. "Instead of using a lot of artificial light, I try to utilize natural light. This is an artistic decision, but also makes the dog more comfortable," he says. "In today's society, people interact less and less with each other. To fill the social gap, dogs play an ever-growing role in our lives. Dogs offer us unconditional love. I think the bond that develops between people and their pets is a huge reason why pet portraits have become something that many dog owners want and wind up cherishing. People don't just want a pretty picture; they want a portrait that captures the unique personality of the animal. That's what sets good pet photography apart."

For someone who wants to take their own photographs of their dog, Dratfield stresses the need for patience. "A dog's eyes are the gateway to their soul. They're honest. You can't rush the photography process. They're not professional models. You can't simply command the dog to pose and smile for a picture. Patience is the key to truly capturing your dog and their personality in a photograph."

Tip When hiring any photographer, it's always smart to preview their work first. (Jim Dratfield's work is showcased on his web site.) If you want a fine art–quality portrait of your dog, find a photographer like Dratfield who specializes exclusively in pet photography. You can find ads for these photographers in upscale pet and dog enthusiast magazines, such as *The New York Dog Magazine*, *The Hollywood Dog Magazine*, *The Bark*, and *Modern Dog*. Many pet supply boutiques can also offer referrals.

Items Featuring Your Dog

Whether you hire a world-renowned pet photographer to shoot portraits of your dog, you visit a portrait center at your mall, or you shoot your own photos, once you have those prints or digital images there are many types of products you can have made to creatively show off your dog to the world.

Custom Photo Collage Canvas

Manufacturer: Exposures
Phone: (800) 222-4947
Web site: www.exposuresonline.com
Availability: Online or via mail order

Supply the designers at Exposures with five color or black-and-white photographs (in any size) of your dog and they'll create a customized and framed canvas photo collage, measuring 26 ½ by 20 ½ inches, which you'll be proud to hang up anywhere.

Your photos will be transformed into stunning black-and-white or sepia images, laid out, transferred to canvas, and then framed. The Custom Collage Canvas costs $229 and is an elegant and creative way to display a handful of your favorite photos of your dog.

Exposures also has a selection of leather-bound photo albums, designer frames, and other custommade products that can be created from photos you supply. Visit the company's web site or request their full-color catalog for details.

A custom-created photo collage on canvas is a wonderful way to display five of your favorite photos of your dog.

Your Dog Everywhere

Using an ordinary color or black-and-white photo, Feron Productions (917-860-3091; www.feron productions.com) will create a nine-image "pop art" collage that's reminiscent of something Andy Warhol would have done. Prices start at $149 for a 20- by 24-inch full-color canvas. Before commissioning the artwork, Feron Productions will e-mail you at no cost a digital sample of what the artwork will look like.

Also using a photo of your dog that you supply, TreasureKnit (416-745-2622; www.treasureknit.com) will create a 50- by 60-inch, full-color, ultrasoft and cozy cotton throw blanket. Prices start at $129.95. Mention *Pampering Your Pooch* and receive a 15% discount when placing an order with TreasureKnit.

Photo Note Cards

Manufacturer: Exposures
Phone: (800) 222-4947
Web site: www.exposuresonline.com
Availability: Online or via mail order

Imagine being able to send your friends, coworkers, and family hand-written notes and letters on custom-printed note cards featuring a color or black-and-white image of your dog. Exposures sells 5- by 7-inch cards with your photo on the front and up to eight lines (twenty-five characters each) of optional custom text inside. Each $39.95 set comes with twenty cards and matching envelopes.

Exposures also has 4 ⅞-inch square note cards with up to four photos on the front, along with a customizable line of text. They cost $34.95 for a set of twenty-four note cards.

You can show off your favorite dog photo on custom note cards.

Custom Photo Notecube

Manufacturer: Exposures
Phone: (800) 222-4947
Web site: www.exposuresonline.com
Availability: Online or via mail order

Show off your favorite dog photo by having it made into a custom photo notecube. This is a great accessory for any dog lover's desk.

On most desks, you'll often find a notepad for jotting down important information. Using a photograph of your dog that you supply, Exposures will create a customized photo notecube, which displays your dog's photo on the sides of the 3 ¼-inch cube, while keeping blank notepaper handy. The Custom Photo Notecube is $19.95. The photograph you supply can be printed on the sides of the notecube in full color, black and white, or sepia.

Create a Scrapbook for Your Dog

Throughout your dog's life, there will be moments you'll want to remember forever. Consider documenting those important moments by creating a scrapbook for your dog.

Creating a scrapbook can be as easy as putting a handful of photographs in an album and adding dates and captions, or can become an ongoing project that taps your creativity as you incorporate pieces of memorabilia, photos, and other items into an album where each page tells a story or captures a chapter in your dog's life. To find the albums and scrapbooking materials you'll need, visit any art or photo supply store.

Scrapbook.com sells a wide range of scrapbooking products, plus how-to articles, sample page layouts, and other resources for first-time and experienced scrapbookers alike. Use the search phrase "dog" to find a wide range of scrapbook items with canine themes.

The Exposures catalog (800-222-4947; www.exposuresonline.com) also has a handful of high-end, leather-bound photo and scrapbook albums.

Photo Checks

Manufacturer: Unique Products
Phone: (888) 824-3257
Web site: www.uniquechecks.com/Home.aspx
Availability: Online

A number of check supply companies—often including your own bank—offer designer checks. These checks might have a special color scheme or precreated design that lets you show off your personality as you pay your bills. Taking this concept a step further, a handful of companies sell customized photo checks. Using your favorite photograph of your dog, you can have checks printed that feature Fido's furry face.

Unique Checks is just one company that custom-prints checks with a photograph you supply. When ordering checks, you'll need to send in a color photograph, along with your name and address, bank name, checking account number, and your bank's routing number. This is all information displayed on your current checks. Personalized photo checks start at $19.95 per box. Each box contains 150 checks. Matching address labels can also be ordered.

Other companies that print customized photo checks include:

✦ American Bank Checks: www.americanbankchecks.com

✦ Carousel Checks: www.carouselchecks.com

✦ MyPhotoChecks: www.myphotochecks.com

Photo Mugs, Mouse Pads, and Other Fun Gifts

Using your photographs, many companies can create a wide range of fun products, including coffee mugs, T-shirts, mouse pads, photo greeting cards, puzzles, and even Christmas ornaments that display your favorite photos. These products make great gifts, they're relatively inexpensive, plus they're a fun way to treat yourself, especially if you have a favorite picture of your dog that you'd like to show off.

These products can be ordered from almost any local photo processing shop, or online from one of these services:

✦ America Online's You've Got Pictures: Click on the 'Photos' icon on the main American Online Welcome screen (for AOL members only)

✦ CafePress: www.cafepress.com

✦ Kodak EasyShare Gallery: www.kodakgallery.com

- ◆ Photo Pet Gifts: www.photopetgifts.com
- ◆ ShutterFly: www.shutterfly.com
- ◆ Snapfish: www.snapfish.com

Canine Customizing Your Computer Desktop

Whether you have a computer at work or at home, you can customize the desktop and the screen saver using your favorite dog photos. It's a fun and easy way to view photos of your dog as you're using your computer and working throughout the day. Begin by transferring photos of your dog to your computer in digital form. (If you don't take digital pictures, you can have your photo prints scanned at your local one-hour photo-processing center, camera shop, or at a Kinko's or similar place.)

Next, if you're using Windows XP, go to your main desktop and right-click the mouse. Choose "Properties" from the menu that appears. To modify your desktop, from the "Display Properties" menu, select "Desktop" and choose the photo of your choice from where it's stored on your computer's hard drive. Do this by clicking on the "Browse" icon. Select your favorite photo and it will then appear as the wallpaper on your main desktop screen.

Using Windows XP, you can also create a customized screen saver using a handful of your favorite dog photos. From the "Properties" menu, select "Screen Saver." When you see the "Display Properties" screen, select "My Picture Slideshow" from the pull-down menu. Click on the "Settings" icon to determine the directory where your digital images are stored and choose the photos you want displayed. From the "My Pictures Screen Saver Option," you can decide how long each picture will be displayed, how large each will appear on your computer screen, and whether fancy animated transitions will be used as the photos are displayed.

For more detailed, step-by-step directions on how to do this using a PC computer running Windows XP, visit the web site www.limowiz.com/customizing_desktop_notebook.htm.

You can also customize the desktop and screen saver on Macintosh computers. For step-by-step directions, point your web browser to www.ali.apple.com/ali_sites/adcchd/Exhibits/Assets/unit_basics_panther/BS_2_Step_WorkWDesktop.pdf.

Real U.S. Postage Stamps with Your Dog's Photo

PhotoStamps.com (www.photostamps.com) lets you transform your favorite photo into actual first class postage stamps accepted by the United States Postal Service. To order stamps, simply upload your photo to the company's web site and complete the order form. The price of one sheet, containing twenty first class stamps, is $17.99 plus shipping. Quantity discounts are available.

Showcase your favorite dog photo on your computer's desktop and with your screensaver.

Nintendogs: A Video Game for All Dog Lovers

Who says video games are just for kids? One of the more innovative video games is designed for dog lovers of all ages and available for the Nintendo DS handheld video game system. Nintendogs (800-255-3700; www.nintendo.com) is a very realistic simulator that lets you adopt an extremely life-like virtual dog, raise him, interact with him, and train him.

You can choose the breed of dog you want to adopt (such as Chihuahua, German Shepherd Dog, Boxer, Yorkshire Terrier, or Cavalier King Charles Spaniel), then spend countless hours interacting with your dog using the video game system's stylus and tapping the screen or using voice commands. The Nintendo DS system can respond to your voice when you speak into the built-in microphone. For this game, you can use your dog's name (which you provide) and say commands such as "Fido sit" or "Fido roll over." Part of this simulation involves virtual feeding and walking your dog, giving him toys, grooming him, and teaching him tricks.

Nintendogs is a dog simulation game for the popular Nintendo DS handheld video game system. In the game, you adopt, raise, and train an extremely lifelike virtual dog.

More than 2 million copies of Nintendogs have been sold worldwide. This is an extremely realistic and fun way to interact with a virtual dog when you're commuting to work or traveling and can't be with your own dog. There are three separate versions of the Nintendogs game ($29.99 each), each with a handful of breeds to adopt, and the Nintendo DS video game system ($129.99). All are sold separately and are available wherever video games are sold.

Knit Your Way into Your Dog's Heart

While your dog probably won't know the difference between a store-bought sweater and one you knit or crochet yourself, you'll know that your love and hard work went into something you made by hand for your dog. If you know how to knit, crochet, or sew, there are many patterns you can get to make creating your own doggy sweater easier. You can even create a matching sweater or scarf for yourself.

The following web sites have free knitting or crochet patterns for making a doggy sweater:

✦ http://knitting.about.com/library/ndogcoat.htm

✦ www.cs.oswego.edu/~ebozak/knit/esb-patterns/dog-sweater.html

✦ www.doggoneknit.com/patterns/crochet/onepiecesolid.html

✦ www.knitlist.com/99gift/carolines-dog-sweater.htm

✦ www.lionbrand.com/patterns/kff-dogSweater.html

✦ www.nakedsheep.com/patdogsweatp.html

✦ www.redlipstick.net/knit/chihswe.html

8

Carriers and Crates

Transport Your Dog in Style

*I*f your dog is like many dogs, she probably enjoys going out—not just for walks, but wherever you go. If you have a big dog, you can choose a fashionable collar and leash (see chapter 4) to show off your taste and hers. If she's small, it's okay to carry her in a designer bag, as long as she's comfortable and not simply being used, like a pair of earrings or a scarf, to complement your outfit. Remember, your dog is not a fashion accessory! She's a living creature who loves you and wants to be loved. Your most important consideration is choosing the very best carrier for your dog, to meet her needs and yours.

Especially if you have a small dog, there are dozens of designer carriers and bags available that will enable you to take your dog along in fine style. As you'll discover, some carriers are designed for specific purposes, such as keeping your dog safe when riding in the car.

Choosing the Perfect Carrier

Carriers come in many shapes, colors, and styles, and range in price from $30 to more than $20,000. Depending on your needs (and your dog's), you may find it necessary to buy two or three carriers for your dog. For example, you might want a purselike carrier for everyday use, an airline-approved carrier for when you fly, and a car seat or carrier that will keep your dog safe while traveling in your car.

To help you find the perfect carrier for your dog, this chapter breaks these important pet accessories into four basic types.

✦ Purselike carriers are ideal for transporting your dog around town and carrying her with you on your shoulder. Because they resemble purses or handbags, they more often appeal to female dog owners.

- Traditional soft-sided carriers are the most popular, because they're suitable for bringing your dog in the car, aboard an airplane (within the cabin), and for general travel. They're usually rectangular, are the most versatile, and come in many designs, sizes, and color schemes.

- Hard-bodied crates have a variety of uses. They're more cumbersome than soft-sided carriers, but are necessary if your dog will be traveling in the pressurized cargo hold of an airplane. They're also more practical for medium and large dogs.

- Doggy car seats and harnesses are ideal for keeping your dog safe while traveling in the car.

One of the things you'll discover when you start shopping for quality pet carriers is that few are truly well designed (with the dog's safety and comfort in mind), manufactured from top-quality materials, *and* fashionable. For dog owners who consider themselves to be on the cutting edge of fashion, there are several carrier manufacturers, including Posh Pooch, Gucci, Louis Vuitton, and Aurora, that have high-end products ideal for transporting dogs under 15 pounds. Sherpa Pet Trading Company also has a variety of carriers that are midpriced but extremely well designed and highly functional.

Tip Always measure your dog from head to tail and know her weight *before* you shop for a carrier. If your dog is still growing, plan for that growth or be prepared to buy a new carrier when she gets older.

One of the biggest mistakes dog owners make is focusing on the designer label or the look of the carrier, as opposed to its functionality and how well it suits their particular dog. Showing off your style and flare for fashion with a designer carrier that matches your purse, outfit, or luggage is fine, as long as the carrier is also well designed for your dog and provides a safe and comfortable environment.

As a pet owner, your first and foremost concern must always be for the comfort and safety of your dog. Before buying a carrier, ask yourself the following questions:

- How will the carrier be used? Will it primarily be a shoulder bag or a purse for carrying your dog? Will it be used for safely transporting your dog in the car or on an airplane?

- How much time will your dog be spending in the carrier?

- What is your dog's size and weight and what size carrier do you need? It's always better to buy a slightly larger carrier than you need to ensure your dog's comfort.

- What features do you want on the carrier? Are a shoulder strap or wheels important? Do you want a soft-sided carrier or a hard-bodied, cratelike carrier?

- Does the carrier have a waterproof lining, especially around the inside and bottom of the bag?

- Is the carrier and/or lining washable?

- Does the carrier have pockets for storing a leash, treats, a small water bottle, or a toy?

+ How heavy is the bag? Will you be able to carry it easily with your dog inside?

+ Can the carrier easily be strapped into your car with a seat belt to keep your dog secure while you're driving?

+ If you'll be traveling by airplane with a small dog (under 15 pounds), does the carrier meet airline specifications and easily fit under an airplane seat? (See chapter 13 for more information about traveling with your dog.)

The actual construction of the carrier is important. Look at the quality of the zippers, the metal hardware and straps, how well the bag's seams are stitched, if the bag has adequate ventilation, and whether the bag is well balanced. If your dog curls up on one side of the bag, will the entire bag tilt? Will it always retain its shape?

Tip Before actually using the carrier during your travels, test it out at home to make sure it's the right size for your dog, escape proof, and well constructed.

Carriers for Airplane Travel

If you plan to travel with your dog by airplane, you'll need to follow the guidelines set by the airline you'll be traveling with. These guidelines differ dramatically if you'll be bringing your dog in the cabin with you or if she'll be traveling in a crate in the airplane's pressurized cargo hold.

Carriers that will be brought onto the cabin must easily fit under the seat in front of you and retain their shape (even a soft-sided bag). The required dimensions vary, based on the airline and type of aircraft you'll be flying on. The pet you'll be transporting must weigh less than 15 pounds to accompany you in the cabin. (See chapter 13 for more information about traveling with your pet.)

Carriers that will be placed in the cargo hold of an airplane are considered pet crates, because they must be made of rigid plastic, wood, or metal, have functional handles, and meet a variety of requirements outlined by the individual airlines. All travel crates must be approved by the United States Department of Agriculture (USDA), and must have enough room for your dog to stand and sit erect without her head touching the top of the container. She must also be able to turn around and lie down in a natural position while inside the crate, and have a supply of food and water on hand.

As part of its Delta Pets First program (800-SEND-PET), Delta Air Lines sells pet crates at major U.S. airports that are suitable for flying in the cargo hold. Similar crates are also available from pet supply stores and online pet suppliers.

If your dog will be traveling in the cargo hold, there are certain times of the year when travel isn't permitted because of extreme heat or cold, so check with your airline before booking your flight. And remember, all airlines now charge a fee to travel with your pet. Plus, each flight has a limit on the number of pets that can be traveling within the cabin, so be sure to book your flight early, especially during peak travel times.

Even with soft-sided carriers, make sure the top and sides of the bag are sturdy and won't cave in on your dog. The carrier should always maintain its shape. This is an important feature that some soft-sided dog carrier manufacturers neglected to design into their bags, making them uncomfortable and potentially unsafe for your dog.

If your dog likes to chew, make sure the carrier you choose does not have any accessible tags, Velcro strips, hardware, or zipper tabs on the inside of the bag that could become a choking hazard.

What's great about this PuppyPurse design is that one of the shoulder straps can easily be unhooked and used as a leash.

Purselike Carriers

These carriers are designed to look like a purse or a handbag and also to hold your pet securely and comfortably. They are only suitable for small dogs, and are designed with women in mind. Make sure your purselike carrier is large enough to hold your dog comfortably. Never compromise your dog's comfort and well-being in favor of a smaller, more chic carrier.

PuppyPurse

Price: $70 to $100
Manufacturer: PuppyPurse
Phone: (201) 262-6878
Web site: www.puppypurse.com
Availability: Online and from upscale pet supply boutiques

Although not an enclosed case, this dog harness with shoulder strap enables you to carry your dog like a purse. A PuppyPurse will let your pup ride along at your side, in open-air comfort rather than inside an enclosed carrier. When your dog is being carried in a PuppyPurse, her legs are suspended in midair; the purse wraps around the dog's midsection and stays closed using Velcro.

PuppyPurses are available in a variety of sizes and dozens of fabrics and colors, so they can match any outfit. The solid colors are also suitable for male dog owners. Thanks to easily adjustable straps, you can wear a PuppyPurse like a shoulder bag, a fanny pack, or carry it like a purse.

The PuppyPurses are well made and durable. They work well with any dog under 8 pounds. They're ideal for shorter outings when you and your dog want to be seen around town.

Posh Pooch Carriers

Price: $1,025 to over $20,000
Manufacturer: Posh Pooch
Phone: (718) 874-6064
Web site: www.posh-pooch.com
Availability: Online and from upscale pet supply boutiques

If you're looking for the most fashionable, purselike dog carriers available, the ever-expanding line of Posh Pooch bags offers the ultimate in luxury, top-notch craftsmanship, and high-end design. These bags are handmade in Italy and are truly designed with the pet and her owner in mind.

All Posh Pooch designs maintain their shape and have even weight distribution, even if the dog moves around within the carrier. These carriers come in a wide range of styles and are made from the ultimate in luxurious and exotic materials, including ostrich, alligator, crocodile, stingray, python, and calf skin, and several kinds of leather. They're complemented with solid brass hardware for maximum durability.

Carriers such as the Fushia Plum bag from Posh Pooch are priced from $1,025. The company's most expensive carrier has a $20,000 price tag. Although many of the Posh Pooch carriers resemble high-end purses for women, the company also has several designs that are suitable for men. The company's PP by Posh Pooch line uses leather, suede, faux fur, canvas, and other materials to offer the same glamour and luxury as Posh Pooch, but at more affordable prices.

Giannci Genau is the president of New York City–based Posh Pooch and the company's lead designer. She's a graduate of Parson's School of Design in New York. Every season, Genau expands her line of carriers, based on the latest fashion trends. With bags that are so beautiful and so well made, it's no wonder some of Hollywood's biggest celebrities have added a Posh Pooch bag to their personal collection.

According to Genau, "I was a sophomore in college when I came up with the idea for Posh Pooch. It has since evolved into a company that sells some of the finest dog carriers anywhere in the world. It's like a Mercedes or Bentley for your dog. The most extravagant bag I've created was made from ostrich, python, and crocodile, then hand painted."

Genau travels all over the world and attends every major fashion event. She then designs her bags to nicely complement the latest designs and fashionable color schemes for each season. "My carriers are on the cutting edge of what's hot each season in terms of fashion," she says.

The Fushia Plum Bag comes in two sizes (14 by 9 ½ by 8 ½ inches and 17 by 10 by 8 ½ inches) and is made from python and calfskin.

The limited edition Fantasie bag from Posh Pooch is one of the company's most expensive designs. Its interior has a waterproof lining, and the exterior is made from a combination of hand-painted python and crocodile skin.

"Dogs are our best friends. I spent over a year developing the core design for our bags to ensure they're comfortable and safe for dogs. Our bags always maintain their shape, for example, which is something that few soft-sided carrier manufacturers can claim. If the dog moves around in the bag, the bag itself will always remain balanced and maintain its shape. The bag's weight is always distributed equally and each has a water-resistant lining, plus a comfortable pillow on the bottom. The majority of my bags are created to look like designer purses, but they're highly functional and comfortable for the dog," she adds. She also suggests finding a carrier that can be secured to a seat when the dog is traveling with you in your car.

When it comes to purses and handbags, Genau has always loved handmade Italian bags, which is why she turned to those same manufacturers to create her line of high-end carriers. She uses the same Italian manufacturers as companies such as Gucci and Prada. "There's a manufacturing technique the Italian craftsmen use that I believe makes their bags superior to those made elsewhere in the world," she says.

Many Posh Pooch bags are custom-designed; these can take anywhere from three to six months to make. "We are a pet fashion house. We offer the same experience someone would have working with a well-known fashion design house if they were to purchase a designer dress," says Genau.

Every season, Posh Pooch introduces new bag designs as well as maintaining a handful of classic favorites, all in a variety of colors and materials. Both Posh Pooch and the lower-priced PP by Posh Pooch also have dog carrier designs that don't look like purses, which are suitable for male dog owners. Many of the bags in the Posh Pooch line can be custom-made in any exotic skin or leather and in any color. Matching collars and leads are also available.

For guys, PP by Posh Pooch's Crème et Chocolat Bag has a more masculine, rectangular design with thick leather straps. It's also more affordable than carriers in the Posh Pooch line.

Pet Totes

Price: $65 to $90
Manufacturer: Sherpa's Pet Trading Company
Phone: (800) 743-7723
Web site: www.sherpapet.net
Availability: Online and from pet supply boutiques and stores nationwide

In addition to its line of more traditional, soft-sided carriers, Sherpa's Pet Trading Company has a line of designer totes featuring more purselike designs. Ideal for women, these totes are available in more than a dozen colors and styles, and in two sizes. The company's totes have durable PVC construction, lockable zippers, mesh panels for ventilation, a padded bottom board for stability, and a washable fleece liner. The Park Avenue pet tote, for example, has an external storage pocket and shoulder straps. This style of carrier is designed to be fashionable but extremely versatile. For a mid-priced bag, it's also exceptionally well made.

Louisbag

Price: $152
Manufacturer: Louisdog
Web site: www.louisdog.com
Availability: Pet supply boutiques nationwide

Available in crayon pink and coffee brown, the Louisbag by Louisdog is one of more than a dozen carriers offered by this designer pet product company. This particular bag has a purselike design. One side has a sealed mesh window and the opposite side has a mesh window that can be fully opened, allowing your dog's head to stick out. A safety ring on the inside of the carrier can be used to keep your dog secured, even with the window open. The top of the bag opens with a zipper. The exterior has several storage pockets.

Juicy Couture Pink and Black Bowler

Price: $275 to $395
Manufacturer: Juicy Couture
Web site: www.juicycouture.com
Availability: Pet supply boutiques nationwide, including Glamourdog.com

Designer Juicy Couture is known around the world for its women's apparel, handbags, shoes, and jewelry. The company also has a growing line of designer pet carriers in a variety of colors and styles. There are more than a dozen carriers to choose from. The Black and Pink Bowler, for example, somewhat resembles a bowling bag in shape. It has a black exterior with pink trim, and is accessorized with sturdy metal hardware. The Juicy logo appears in large pink print on the side of the bag.

This particular carrier opens from the front and the top, and has two mesh sides for the dog to look out and for ventilation. The bag also has several storage pockets. It measures 13 by 7 by 9 inches and is ideal for dogs under 4 ½ pounds.

Carriers made by Juicy Couture come in pink, green, tan, and blue color schemes that are classic Juicy. Matching purses and other accessories, such as iPod cases, are available for some of the more popular styles—all of which are suitable for small dogs. Juicy Couture also has matching leather collar and leash sets (sold separately) for $95 each.

Traditional Soft-Sided Carriers

Louis Vuitton Pet Carrier

Price: $1,400
Manufacturer: Louis Vuitton
Phone: (212) 758-8877
Web site: www.louisvuitton.com
Availability: Visit a Louis Vuitton boutique or an authorized dealer

Louis Vuitton is a well-known name when it comes to high-end designer luggage, handbags, and fashion. Now you can have a genuine Louis Vuitton dog carrier that matches the pieces you already own.

The carrier measures 18 by 13 by 9 inches and comes in a lovely brown-tan color combination. It displays the world-famous LV logo on the exterior canvas. The bag is detailed with cowhide trim and solid brass hardware. It opens from the top and has a large mesh window on either side. The inside of the bag has a waterproof lining for easy cleaning. This bag comes in one size that is suitable for small dogs only.

The Louis Vuitton Pet Carrier was originally released only for a limited time and may not be available from all authorized dealers.

Gucci Dog Bag

Price: $650 to $795
Manufacturer: Gucci
Phone: (212) 826-2600 (New York) or (310) 278-3451 (Beverly Hills)
Web site: www.gucci.com
Availability: Online and from Gucci stores and authorized dealers

This is a lovely carrier that's well constructed and prominently displays the famous Gucci logo on the exterior. Available in three color schemes, this popular carrier has Gucci's signature 9-inch, tricolor web handles, a double-zip side opening, a washable interior cushion, and a short leash clip to hold the dog securely within the bag. The small carrier measures 12 ½ by 7 ⅘ by 9 ⅘ inches, and the larger bag measures 16 ⅖ by 7 ⅘ by 12 ⅒ inches.

> *Tip* If you plan to buy a designer carrier from an online auction web site, beware of counterfeits.

Sherpa Bag Deluxe and Sherpa-on-Wheels

Price: $65 to $145
Manufacturer: Sherpa's Pet Trading Company
Phone: (800) 743-7723
Web site: www.sherpapet.net
Availability: Online and from pet supply stores nationwide

If you're looking for a moderately priced, soft-sided carrier that's versatile, extremely well made, and has the features you'd expect from an expensive carrier, Sherpa has more than twenty-five traditional rectangular styles to choose from. The Sherpa Bag Deluxe is made from quilted nylon and has mesh panels on all sides for ventilation. It can be opened from the side or top. Inside, you'll find a washable faux lambskin liner, while outside are two zippered storage pockets. The Deluxe bag is available in small, medium, large, and extra large and comes in black, navy, green, and red. This bag is great for airline or car travel and makes a perfect everyday carrier.

Sherpa bags offer a lot of quality at a reasonable price.

The Sherpa-on-Wheels has the same basic features as the Deluxe bag, but the four wheels on the bottom make for easy transport. The mesh windows on all four sides provide excellent ventilation and a view for your dog; roll-down flaps can cover these windows to keep the interior warm. The bag has both top and side entry and comes in two sizes, both of which are designed to fit under an airplane seat.

For someone who travels frequently with their dog and wants a durable, highly functional, well-designed, affordable carrier, the Sherpa-on-Wheels is the perfect solution. Carry this bag using its handles, the included shoulder strap, or pull it along on the built-in wheels (a feature that's ideal for navigating your way through airports).

Jacques Traugott Pet Carriers

Price: $96 to $360
Manufacturer: Aurora Pet Products
Phone: (954) 455-0405
Web site: www.aurorapetproducts.com
Availability: Online and from pet supply boutiques nationwide

Aurora Pet Products has more than fifteen Jacques Traugott carrier styles in a variety of colors. Most come in a traditional rectangular design and are made of Napa leather, stamped leather, suede, shearling, cordura fabric, and satin. Most are suitable for airline travel and all have a water-resistant interior lining for easy cleaning. All of the carriers have mesh windows on two or more sides, and most styles come in two or more sizes.

Sports Bag Grand

Price: $93
Manufacturer: Louisdog
Web site: www.louisdog.com
Availability: Pet supply boutiques nationwide

The Sports Bag Grand by Louisdog is designed to look like a sporty gym bag. It has a bright yellow (or pink) and black exterior and is made from a lightweight, water-resistant fabric. The Sports Bag Grand is suitable for men or women and is available in two sizes. One end of the bag has a mesh window that can be fully opened to allow the dog's head to stick out.

The exterior of this carrier has three storage pockets, hand straps, and a removable shoulder strap. Inside the bag is a small leash to hold the dog securely in the bag, and a sturdy padded bottom that's removable for easy cleaning. The entire top of the bag and two sides are solid mesh, providing ventilation and a view for the dog.

Hard-Bodied Crates

Pet supply superstores such as PetCo (www.petco.com) and PetSmart (www.petsmart.com), PetEdge (800-738-3343; www.petedge.com), and virtually every pet supply store in North America, sell a selection of heavy-duty plastic, hard-bodied pet crates in a variety of sizes. Prices range from under $25 to several hundred dollars, depending on size, quality, and features.

When choosing a hard-bodied crate, make sure it's well vented, durable, has strong metal safety gates, is easy to clean, meets airline requirements, has sturdy handles and/or wheels, and is big enough for your dog to stand up and turn around comfortably. There should also be a way to give dog food and water while she's in the crate, using either attachable cups or a bottle (for water).

Keep Cool

Metro Air Force has a battery-powered fan that can be attached to the outside of a hard-bodied pet crate to help keep your dog cool. The fan has two speeds and runs for one hundred hours on two D batteries. It's priced under $15 and is available from PetCo and PetSmart, and at other pet supply stores.

If you'll be flying your dog in the cargo hold of an airplane, make sure you buy Live Animal stickers and a durable identification tag that displays your name and contact information for the outside of the crate.

Popular sizes of hard-bodied crates include:

+ Extra small dogs: 12 to 13 inches wide by 19 to 20 inches deep to 10 to 12 inches high

+ Small dogs: 16 to 17 inches wide by 21 to 24 inches deep by 14 to 16 inches high

+ Medium dogs: 17 to 21 inches wide by 26 to 28 inches deep by 18 to 22 inches high

+ Large dogs: 22 to 26 inches wide by 32 to 36 inches deep by 23 to 28 inches high

+ Extra large dogs: at least 27 inches wide by 40 inches deep by 30 inches high

+ Giant dogs: at least 32 inches wide by 48 inches deep by 35 inches high

Doggy Car Seats

Even though dogs can't wear standard seat belts, it's still important to keep them safe while riding in the car. As a safety precaution for you, your dog, and other motorists, it's never a good idea to drive with a dog on your lap—just as you should never drive holding your infant or young child in your lap. Your dog shouldn't be loose in the car, either, for the same reason your child shouldn't. Plus, your dog can wander around under the seats, impeding your ability to drive safely. And if you're in an accident and a window or door breaks open, you do not want your dog escaping onto a busy road.

If you keep your dog in a carrier in the car, make sure the carrier is buckled or strapped to the car's seat so it won't go flying if you stop short or need to make a sharp turn. An alternative is to purchase a specially designed car seat for your dog. Many let you strap your dog in securely, yet still give her the freedom to look out the car window. When choosing a car seat, make sure you find one that's suitable for your dog's size and weight.

Pet Stow-Away

Price: $89
Manufacturer: Global Pet Products, Inc.
Phone: (800) 338-7392
Web site: www.globalpetproducts.com
Availability: Online and from pet supply boutiques nationwide

Pet Stow-Away is a square carrier that attaches to any seat in your car, using the seatbelt. Using a safety strap that attaches to your dog's leash or harness, the dog is then held within the cushioned seating area of the Pet Stow-Away while traveling. It measures 17 ½ by 15 by 17 ½ inches, is made from sturdy nylon, and has a padded interior where the dog sits.

Because of its open-air design, your dog is free to look out the window and interact with passengers, while she remains securely strapped in. Below the area that holds the dog is a handy storage compartment for keeping your dog's toys and accessories organized while you're on the go. This storage bag also raises the height of the carrier, which enables small dogs to easily look out the car window. This product is designed for small dogs only.

When you reach your destination, the carrier can be taken out and used as a travel bed. When not in use, the carrier folds up to the size of a small suitcase.

Pet Lookout Car Booster Seat

Price: $29 to $39
Manufacturer: Outward House Pet Travel Gear, The Kyjen Company, Inc.
Phone: (800) 477-5735
Web site: www.kyjen.com
Availability: Online and from pet supply boutiques nationwide

The Pet Lookout Car Booster Seat is a relatively inexpensive way to secure your small dog in your car without having to place her in an enclosed carrier. This square booster seat has an open-air design. The seat itself is held in place using your vehicle's seat belt. Using its built-in nylon straps, the Pet Lookout Car Booster Seat takes minutes to install in almost any vehicle. When not in use, it folds up for easy storage.

This product is designed for pets weighing up to 30 pounds. It measures 16 by 15 ½ by 15 ½ inches and is made of durable nylon. A security strap attaches to your dog's collar or harness to keep her in the travel seat. To raise the dog up to window height so she can enjoy her surroundings as you drive, the bottom of the seat has an inflatable booster cushion that raises it up.

For the added safety of your pet, use the Pet Lookout Car Booster Seat with a full body harness. The harness can then be attached to the seat by using the provided strap.

Tip If your open-air car seat or carrier requires you to attach your small dog using a leash, it's safer to attach the leash to a full-body harness, rather than a collar. (See chapter 4 for information on harnesses.)

> **Your Dog's Suitcase**
>
> The Travel Essentials Bag & Kit ($40) from the Kyjen Company (www.kyjen.com) holds essentials for traveling with pets. The bag is not a pet carrier, but is designed to help owners bring along necessary pet gear and keep it organized. It has an elastic opening for easy access to pick-up bags, a secure, removable key holder, and two Port-a-Bowls for food and water. The bag also has several waterproof compartments.

The Kyjen Company makes a wide range of other quality pet products and accessories, including the Walk-and-Go Pet Stroller and the Sling-Go Pet Sling, which hangs on your shoulder, enabling you to comfortably carry a dog weighing up to 20 pounds.

Hug-A-Dog Seatbelt Harness and Doggy Catcher

Price: $24.95 to $52.95
Manufacturer: Hug-A-Dog
Phone: (800) 444-9475
Web site: www.hug-a-dog.com
Availability: Online

Many pet owners are reluctant to use a collar on their small dog. An alternative is to invest in a soft, full-body harness, which many pet experts believe is safer for small dogs.

Hug-A-Dog sells a variety of harness styles in a wide range of sizes and colors, including one style that has a loop through which a seatbelt can be used to secure your dog in the car. This type of harness eliminates the need to place her in an enclosed carrier in the car. You'll find more information about Hug-A-Dog harnesses in chapter 4.

Introducing Your Dog to a New Carrier

As soon as you buy your new carrier, set it up and leave it to air out. When you remove it from its packaging, it may give off a chemical scent for a few days. Let the scent dissipate before you ask your dog to go inside.

When the carrier is ready to use, introduce your dog to it slowly. One way to do this is to leave it open on the floor and allow your dog to examine and smell it carefully, before you attempt to put her in. To help your dog feel comfortable in her new surroundings, you could put her favorite blanket or toy in the carrier or put in an old T-shirt that you have worn (and that still holds your scent) to make your pet feel safe.

Never confine your dog in the carrier to discipline her. She needs to feel like being put into the carrier and going out with you is a reward. She should look forward to traveling with you and spending time in her carrier.

No matter how nice the carrier is, it will take time for your dog to become accustomed to it, so be patient. Don't simply buy a new carrier, put your dog inside, then head to the airport to take her on a long flight.

9

Health Insurance

Be Prepared for Emergencies

There are countless ways to show your dog how much you love him. You can rub his belly, give him a treat, take him for a run in the park, play fetch, or cuddle up on the couch to watch television with him. Your dog will appreciate and love you for all of the time you spend with him. Of course, you can also pamper your dog with all kinds of products and services, like the ones you've been reading about throughout this book.

One of the most important investments you can make in the well-being of your pampered pooch is health insurance. Just as people have health insurance to help ease the financial burden of medical emergencies and illness, health insurance for your dog can be an extremely worthwhile investment to ensure he gets the best care whenever it's needed. For about the same price as one month's premium for your own health insurance (often less), your dog can be protected for an entire year. For an investment of about $1 a day, you can have peace of mind knowing your dog is covered for most types of illnesses and medical emergencies.

If your dog gets lost or stolen, there are also several ways to help ensure his prompt return. Later in this chapter you'll discover why having your dog microchipped is worthwhile. Also, by registering your dog with a service like Help-4-Pets, you increase your chances of having him promptly returned if he gets lost.

What Is Pet Insurance?

Pet insurance works just like health insurance for people. It covers a significant portion of your dog's medical bills resulting from accidents and illness, and some policies also cover routine care, veterinary office visits, prescriptions, diagnostic tests, X-rays, and lab fees. Depending on the insurance plan you choose, surgeries, cancer treatments, hospitalization, and heartworm protection may also be covered.

Your personal finances are the last thing you want to be worrying about when your dog needs medical treatment, such as emergency surgery (which can cost several thousand dollars). With insurance, your veterinarian can pursue the best medical treatments available without cost becoming a deciding factor.

Insurance for your pet works much like a traditional health insurance policy for humans. Your dog can see any licensed veterinarian, anywhere in the world. You pay a monthly or annual premium for your dog's insurance. Then, you follow these steps when he needs medical care:

1. Bring your dog to any licensed veterinarian or animal hospital.

2. At the time of the office visit or emergency medical care, you pay for the necessary treatments.

3. Have the veterinarian complete a claim form provided by the health insurance company.

4. Sign and mail (or fax) the insurance claims form with your veterinarian's invoice to the insurance company.

5. Within two to four weeks, you'll receive a reimbursement check from the insurance company, based on the amount of insurance coverage you've purchased.

Pet Health Insurance Companies

When shopping for pet insurance, consider the price of the monthly or annual premiums, but more important, focus on what services are covered by the insurance, the dollar amount of coverage offered, and how quickly you'll be reimbursed for out-of-pocket medical expenses. Finally, consider the maximum annual benefit offered by the policy and make sure it's adequate to cover major emergencies or long-term illnesses.

Before choosing a coverage plan, make sure you know what's not covered. For example, preexisting conditions, medical issues associated with pregnancy or breeding, congenital conditions, and some specific diseases are not covered by most pet insurance plans. The insurance company or your veterinarian can help you analyze your coverage needs.

Five of the more popular and well-established pet insurance companies in the United States are:

✦ AKC Pet Healthcare Plan: (866) 725-2747; www.akcpethealthcare.com

✦ Pet Plan Insurance: (800) 268-1169; www.petplan.com

✦ Pet's Best: (877) 738-7237; www.petsbest.com

✦ Pets Health Care Plan: (800) 884-6409; www.petshealthplan.com

✦ VPI Pet Insurance: (800) 872-7387; www.petinsurance.com

How to Sign Up Your Dog

Signing up your dog for pet insurance takes just minutes. Simply call the toll-free phone number for one of the popular pet insurance companies or visit the company's web site and register online. Coverage can begin immediately.

When registering your dog, you'll need to provide his name, breed, date of birth, and date of adoption. You'll also need to review the various coverage plans offered by the insurance company, then choose the appropriate plan for your dog and decide if you'd like to pay your premiums monthly or annually.

How Much Does It Cost?

Depending on the level of coverage you desire and the age of your pet when you sign up, insurance will cost anywhere from $300 to $600 a year.

Tip Some pet insurance companies will not increase your annual premium for the life of your dog, if your sign your dog up before he reaches age 9 and maintain the coverage. For the lowest premiums, it's best to register your dog when he's a puppy.

Have Your Dog Microchipped

If your dog gets lost and is not wearing his collar, or the collar somehow comes off, he could be brought to the nearest animal shelter and given up for adoption, or even put to death if you don't locate him quickly. According to HomeAgain Pet Recovery Service, one in three pets in the United States will get lost. Without proper identification, 90 percent won't return home. Every year, 10 million pets become lost or separated from their owners. Most arrive in shelters with no collar or identification.

One way to permanently identify your dog, even if he's not wearing an ID tag, is microchipping. This popular method will help ensure your dog can be identified and returned to you if he ever gets lost. A microchip is a tiny transponder encased in a bubble of strong, smooth, biocompatible glass that's about the size of a grain of rice. Using a syringe, a veterinarian will insert the chip under the skin on your dog's shoulder, where it will safely remain forever. (Once inserted, your dog will not feel the chip.)

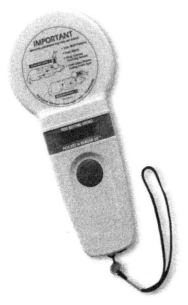

Most veterinarians, animal hospitals, and shelters have a handheld microchip scanner like this one.

Each transponder has a unique number. To retrieve this number, a special handheld scanner is passed over the dog's shoulder. However, the number by itself has no meaning. You must register the chip number with a microchip recovery service. Once registered, your dog's chip number is stored in a database with your contact information. So, if you move or change your phone number, it's vital to keep these records up-to-date with the microchip recovery service you're registered with.

Your veterinarian will charge you a one-time fee to insert the microchip (usually less than $100). You will then have to pay a fee to the microchip recovery service, which may have to be renewed annually (depending on the service).

Unfortunately, there's no single centralized database for registering your dog's information, so whoever finds your dog may have to call around to several services before they find you. There's also no single standard for the manufacture of microchips, and not all scanners will read all chips. Legislation is currently being proposed to establish a universal identification system, and already several scanner manufacturers have made devices that can read chips from other companies.

HomeAgain Pet Recovery Service

Price: Under $75
Manufacturer: Schering-Plough Animal Health
Phone: (800) 521-5767
Web site: www.homeagainid.com
Availability: Contact your veterinarian

HomeAgain Pet Recovery Service makes a microchip that can be read using a Universal HomeAgain Scanner (a device most veterinarians and animal shelters are equipped with).

More than 6 million dogs have been microchipped so far, 3 million of whom are enrolled and registered with the HomeAgain Recovery System, according to the company. The chip and initial registration cost about $75. If you adopt a dog who has already been microchipped with a HomeAgain chip, the cost to register the chip is under $25.

Avid MicroChip/PETtrac

Price: Under $100
Manufacturer: Avid Microchip ID Systems
Phone: (800) 336-2843
Web site: www.avidmicrochip.com
Availability: Contact your veterinarian

Avid MicroChip supplies veterinarians, kennels, animal hospitals and shelters with the equipment needed to inject microchips into pets and retrieve information stored on the chips using a handheld reader. The company also operates the PETtrac Recovery System, which is available twenty-four hours a day. The service is available for animals who have the Avid chip. This chip is readable by cross-compatible scanners.

When an Avid microchip is located in an animal, PETtrac will give the shelter, animal control officer, or veterinarian your name and contact information.

AKC Companion Animal Recovery

Price: $12.50 for the chip registration
Manufacturer: American Kennel Club
Phone: (800) 252-7894
Web site: www.akccar.org
Availability: Online

Founded in 1995, the AKC Companion Animal Recovery Service will register any brand of microchip, tattoo, or specially numbered AKC tag or collar. For a one-time fee of $12.50, your contact information will be permanently stored in the database and be available to kennels, shelters, veterinarians, animal hospitals, and other authorities, twenty-four hours a day. The enrollment process takes just minutes and can be done online using a major credit card. So far, AKC Companion Animal Recovery Service has registered more than 3 million pets and has helped with the safe recovery of more than 300,000 animals, according to the company.

Added Protection for Your Dog

Help-4-Pets

Price: $20 a year
Manufacturer: Help-4-Pets
Phone: (800) HELP-4-PETS
Web site: www.help4pets.com
Availability: Online

Most traditional dog tags list nothing more than your dog's name and one contact phone number. And even microchip recovery services only list one or two contact names. But what happens if your dog gets lost and you're not home? Help-4-Pets is a low-cost service that will track you down in case of emergency, plus coordinate and approve emergency medical care for your dog until you're reached. It's like a 9-1-1 service for dogs.

The services offered by Help-4-Pets are not a replacement for pet insurance or for proper identification. They are an additional service that could prove extremely beneficial, however. For $20 a year (plus a one-time $5 registration fee), you can make sure your dog will receive the help he needs if he gets lost or injured when you're not around.

When you register your dog with Help-4-Pets (a service that was founded in 1996), you'll receive a small identification tag imprinted with the Help-4-Pets toll-free phone number and your dog's

---

Safety at Night

When walking your dog at night, it's smart to carry a bright flashlight, not just to see where you're going, but to make sure oncoming cars will see you and your dog. Also, keep your dog close to you, especially if you're walking along a road. Some collars and harnesses are made with special reflective material that can easily be spotted when a light reflects off them. But don't use any collar with a flashing light that might shine in your dog's eyes. Brookstone's Microbeam Hands-Free light ($30, item no. 431437) is a small but powerful clip-on flashlight that can be worn on your clothing. It emits a bright white light or a flashing red light that can be seen from a distance. It's available online (www.brookstone.com) or from any Brookstone store.

unique ID number. If your dog is lost or injured, anyone who finds him can call the phone number on the tag and Help-4-Pets will call you at home, work, and on your pager or cell phone, plus call up to four other people you have designated until someone is reached. If your dog needs emergency medical care in the meantime, the Help-4-Pets representative will assist the person who finds your injured dog in locating either your dog's own veterinarian or an emergency medical center nearby, and then make sure the necessary treatment is approved.

The Help-4-Pets service keeps on file your dog's complete medical history (provided by you), including details about allergies and medications, which will be promptly forwarded to emergency care providers.

Help-4-Pets' toll-free hotline is available twenty-four hours a day, seven days a week, and is also an excellent resource when you're traveling with your dog and need emergency assistance. From Help-4-Pets, you can obtain emergency veterinary referrals anywhere in the United States, plus travel protection, natural disaster assistance, and home emergency assistance.

Once your dog is registered with Help-4-Pets, adding the service's special ID tag to your dog's collar will help ensure his quick return if he gets lost anywhere in the country.

Another benefit offered to members is a bright-colored sticker that can be placed on your front door or window, informing emergency personnel that a dog lives in your home.

When it's not an emergency, Help-4-Pets can also provide local referrals for pet sitters, behaviorists, and lawyers who specialize in pet cases. You can also learn about pet-friendly hotel accommodations nationwide, plus receive expert advice on adopting a new dog.

Registering your dog with Help-4-Pets takes minutes and can be done over the phone or from the service's web site. If you travel with your dog or you have concerns that your dog could get loose and become lost, this is an extremely worthwhile service.

Be Prepared for Emergencies *Before* They Happen

While it's impossible to predict when an emergency will arise, preparation and planning will make most emergencies a little easier to deal with. If your dog is involved in an accident or gets lost or stolen, has a medical emergency, or suddenly becomes ill, having basic supplies on hand and knowing exactly how to handle the emergency can help make sure emergencies don't end in tragedy.

Supplies You Should Have on Hand

Below is a checklist of items you should have handy for your dog in case of emergency. Consider packing these items in a waterproof or weather-resistant overnight bag and keeping it in your home or vehicle. Be prepared to take these items with you if you need to evacuate your home or deal with some type of emergency:

+ Dog food and water (at least a forty-eight-hour supply)

+ Dog crate and leash

+ Dog toy

+ Blanket

+ Medications your dog is currently taking

+ Pet first aid kit

+ Flashlight

+ Copies of your dog's medical and vaccination records and insurance information

+ The name, phone number, and address of your dog's veterinarian, plus a local animal hospital that's open twenty-four hours a day, seven days a week. Have driving directions to these locations preprinted. Completing the Pet Emergency Information Sheet (page 126) at the end of this chapter will help you gather the necessary information and keep it easily available.

+ A recent photo of your dog to show to authorities or emergency personnel if he gets lost or stolen

Many pet supply stores sell prepackaged pet first aid kits. Practical Trauma (www.practical trauma.com/pet.html), for example, sells a comprehensive first aid kit for pets that's priced at $35. Quake Kare (800-2-PREPARE; www. quakekare.com/survival_kit_pskdk.html) has a Dog Emergency Survival Kit for $39.95.

Tip In addition to offering pet first aid courses at Red Cross centers throughout the country, the American Red Cross Store (www.redcross.org) sells its own 111-page illustrated book that covers how to deal with more than fifty pet emergency medical situations. *The Pet First Aid Book* ($12.95, item no. RC657102-G) is a great resource for all dog owners.

The Pet Emergency Information Sheet

On page 126 you'll find a comprehensive Pet Emergency Information Sheet. Fill in the information and keep copies of this sheet in your home and car, plus in your pet first aid kit. Having this information available when you need it could save valuable time when there's an emergency and time is of the essence.

Pet Emergency Information Sheet

Dog's name: _____

Birth date: _____

Sex: _____

Breed: _____

Weight: _____

Measurements: _____

Known allergies/medical conditions: _____
_____

Breeder contact information: _____

Veterinarian Information

Veterinarian's name: _____

Phone number: _____

Address: _____
_____

Driving directions from home: _____
_____

24-Hour Animal Hospital

Name: _____

Phone number: _____

Address: _____
_____

Driving directions from home: _____

_____

Dog License

Local dog license information
Town/city/state issued:_____

ID number: _____

Pet Insurance

Pet insurance company:_____

Phone number: _____

Policy number/account number: _____

Microchip

Microchip company:_____

Phone number: _____

Microchip ID number: _____

Help-4-Pets

Help-4-Pets: (800) HELP-4-PETS / www.Help4Pets.com
ID number: _____

(Attach a recent photo of your dog to this form and keep it readily available.)

10

Dog Massage and Pet Psychics

Zen and the Art of Pampering Your Pooch

*S*ome people are spa junkies. They truly enjoy being pampered with massages, body wraps, facials, and a wide range of other luxurious treatments. A visit to a day spa can dramatically help someone calm their entire body and mind, release their stress, and relax.

It's no secret that a massage can be highly therapeutic and extremely relaxing, whether someone suffers from a physical ailment or is rehabilitating from an injury. So, if this type of treatment is both beneficial and enjoyable to a human, it makes perfect sense that a pampered dog should also be able to enjoy the benefits and relaxation of a good massage. After all, most dogs often suffer from stress and anxiety, too.

This chapter is all about massage and Reiki treatments for dogs. It also explores the potential benefits of working with a pet psychic to help you better understand and communicate with your canine friend.

The Benefits of Pet Massage

Although the day-to-day stresses your dog experiences are very different from the ones you experience, the impact of that stress on her mind and body can be the same. Pet massage and the massage you'd receive at an upscale day spa are extremely similar, in terms of the actual treatment, procedures, and benefits. It's important to understand, however, that while the law dictates that a massage therapist for people must be trained and licensed in their state, this is *not* the case for pet massage therapists. There are several established and accredited schools that teach pet massage. However, there are no laws requiring that someone who calls themselves a "pet massage therapist" be a graduate of any type of formal training, certification, or licensing program.

The best-qualified pet massage therapists have undergone training to be a human massage therapist, plus have received additional instruction on how to work with animals. It's extremely important to find someone who has the appropriate training and experience to work with your dog.

Jonathan Rudinger, a registered nurse and licensed massage therapist (for humans), is the founder and president of PetMassage (800-779-1001; www.petmassage.com), based in Toledo, Ohio. It is one of the country's leading massage therapy schools for people who want to work with animals. Rudinger has trained thousands of people to become professional dog massage therapists.

"I grew up riding horses and later participated in competitions," says Rudinger. "When any of my horses got injured, I wound up massaging them to aid in their recovery. This was back in 1982. In 1997, I appeared on a television show to demonstrate my work with horses and was asked to work on a dog as well. I applied some of the same techniques and quickly saw tremendous results."

After spending considerable time fine-tuning his massage techniques for dogs, Rudinger developed a training program for massage therapists who are interested in working with all breeds of dogs. He has since written several instructional books and produced training DVDs, plus continues to teach in-person, weeklong workshops focusing on massage and energy work for dogs.

Jonathan Rudinger, the founder of PetMassage, has trained more than 4,000 people to become dog massage therapists.

A massage for a human will often be very similar to a dog's massage. "What I have discovered is that when I massage a dog with a tender muscle, for example, they'll react immediately," Rudinger says.

Depending on where you live, the cost of a dog massage can range from $25 to $150 per session. "When looking for a massage therapist for your dog, make sure they've been properly trained and have experience," Rudinger advises. "When someone joins the International Association of Animal Massage & Bodywork, it means they've adopted the organization's code of ethics, plus they have been properly trained. I'd also look for someone who has a good heart and who has the ability to connect and interact well with your pet."

He continues, "To be a successful massage therapist for dogs, it's necessary to understand how animals communicate, their behavior, and their psychology. There's a certain way for the massage therapist to stand, approach the animal, manage eye contact, and work with the dog. The therapist's body language is extremely important for calming the dog during a massage therapy session."

When Rudinger works with a dog, he begins by taking the dog's medical history. During this time, he'll be watching the dog and how she interacts with her owner. This gives Rudinger a sense of the dog he'll be working with. "Providing a massage to a dog requires the therapist to figure out what is needed. It involves developing an understanding of each dog's unique needs and personality," he says.

Tip The International Association of Animal Massage & Bodywork (800-903-9350; www.iaamb.org) is a nonprofit, professional association comprised of massage therapists who have undergone special training to work with animals, including dogs. This organization can provide referrals for a qualified massage therapist for your dog.

He then lifts the dog onto his specially designed massage table and begins calming the dog by practicing breathing techniques and meditation. At this point, Rudinger places both of his hands on the animal and begins his carefully orchestrated massage sequence—a thirty- to forty-five-minute session during which the dog often falls asleep.

"A massage session works every muscle group of the dog and also serves as cardio exercise," he says. "A massage will improve a dog's circulation, lymphatic flow, and flexibility, plus help the dog get used to being around people. It'll also increase the flow of energy throughout the dog's body."

Just as upscale day spas for people use mood lighting, aromatherapy, and calming music to create a relaxing space where the massage will take place, Rudinger believes the same type of environment benefits dogs. "I always play the same calming music when I massage a dog. This helps communicate to the dog that she's about to be massaged and begins to calm her right away.

"The first few sessions will be a bit confusing for the dog. After several sessions, because dogs are a creature of habit, by the time she pulls up in the parking lot with her owner and realizes she's about to get a massage, you'll actually be able to see the dog physically relax even before a session begins," says Rudinger.

If you live in or plan to visit the Toledo, Ohio, area, Rudinger has established the PetMassage Health and Fitness Center (419-475-4333), a full-service spa and fitness center for dogs. Its facilities include a large indoor, heated swimming pool where canine water massage treatments are done. The fitness center also has many other types of exercise equipment and specially designed exercises that work out a dog's entire body.

Do It Yourself

Rudinger believes strongly that all dog owners should learn basic pet massage techniques they can use on their own dog. When a pet owner massages their dog, it dramatically helps solidify the human-canine bond, plus it relaxes the dog. "Massage can also be a wonderful bonding experience between the dog and her owner, if the owner is the one doing the massage," says Rudinger. "I have also seen dogs work through a wide range of emotional problems and anxieties as a result of regular massages. Ideally, I like to see massage used in conjunction with formal dog training."

Dog massage works well on any size and breed of dog, regardless of age. "Every animal needs to be touched. For owners who massage their own dogs, this is something that can be done every day or several times per week," Rudinger adds. "The thing to remember, however, is to avoid getting too rough when massaging your dog. Also, the massage session should be about calming, healing, and grounding. It should be a controlled session and not mixed with play time."

If you're interested in learning how to massage your dog, Rudinger has created a home study course that is suitable for any dog owner. The home study course is a scaled-down version of the extensive training program offered to people interested in becoming professional dog massage therapists. It includes a full-length book and two DVDs. Most people can get through the entire course in several hours and give their dog her first massage the same day.

The PetMassage home study course is priced around $50. PetMassage also manufactures a padded dog massage bed that costs $325.

Reiki for Dogs Focuses on Energy

An alternative to massage therapy that is gaining popularity among humans is Reiki. What is Reiki? It's an ancient Tibetan Buddhist form of energy medicine that was revived in the nineteenth century by a Japanese physician and Buddhist monk named Hichau Mikao Usui and was introduced to the West in 1990 by a Japanese Hawaiian, Hawayo Tokata. Practitioners claim to serve as a conduit for universal life energy (known as *qi*). They lay their hands on a patient and believe the energy flows through their palms to specific parts of the body to facilitate healing.

Reiki is said to reduce stress, improve general health and quality of life, and help heal physical and emotional ailments. Scientific studies have not confirmed the existence of Reiki energy, but practitioners claim great benefits. And if it's good for you, why not let your dog in on it?

Sharel Groome (deerpath7@hotmail.com) is a Massachusetts-based Certified Reiki Master, animal communicator, Certified Equine Sports Massage Therapist, and state and federally licensed rehabilitator. She has grown up around animals and regularly practices both massage and Reiki on humans, dogs, horses, and other animals.

"I love animals," Groome says. "I began working with them professionally after completing a certification course in equine massage. This taught me that I needed to learn more. I started out working on horses, but later began learning about working with dogs as well. I have learned a series or sequence of techniques that I use on dogs that hits all of their pressure points."

She continues, "Reiki is an ancient technique that uses energy to promote healing. It's not at all like a traditional massage, because physical touch is seldom used. The hands are used to transfer energy."

Groome approaches each of her animal clients differently, based on their needs and personalities. "It's a little different than working on a person, because a person can tell you exactly where they're sore, so you can work on those specific areas," she explains.

A typical Reiki session involves working one-on-one with the animal, with soothing music playing in the background. "I don't use a massage table; I lay a quilt out on the floor. A typical session lasts between thirty and sixty minutes. By the time the session ends, almost all of the dogs are extremely relaxed," says Groome.

She believes we live in a stressful world and that in addition to the normal stresses in an animal's life, many pets pick up on the stress experienced by their owners. People go to massage therapists and for Reiki because they need downtime to relax their minds and bodies. The benefits dogs experience from these treatments are very similar to those a human experiences.

Based on Groome's experience, massage for dogs works best on muscle-related issues and has very little impact on joints. She believes that working dogs (those who appear in dog shows, for example), should be massaged once a week. Other dogs will benefit from weekly, semiweekly, or monthly treatments.

When it comes to finding a Reiki practitioner, Groome believes it's important to find someone who has been trained as a Certified Reiki Master and who also has training working with animals. "Referrals from veterinarians, groomers, kennels, or pet supply shops are often useful, but dog owners should be careful because most states don't require practitioners or therapists to be licensed to work on dogs," says Groome. "A lot of people want to pamper their pets and believe that pet massage or Reiki is a frivolous thing. While treatments *are* a way to pamper your pet, they have very positive and calming benefits as well."

Need Help Understanding Your Dog? Try a Pet Psychic

This next section focuses on pet psychics—people who believe they can telepathically communicate with animals. Is there anything to this? Well, that's up to you to decide for yourself. Thousands of pet owners have sought out the help of psychics to communicate with their dogs. Some people use psychics to communicate with dogs who have passed away, while others are more concerned about what their living dog is really thinking.

Pet psychics work the same way as psychics who work with people. Most tap into energy, feelings, images, or sounds they see and hear as a result of their special abilities. Terri Jay (www.terrijay.com) is a psychic from Reno, Nevada, who works with people as well as pets. Jay also does a lot of grief counseling for pet owners who have recently experienced loss.

While some psychics insist they need to be in close proximity to the client they're working with, Jay says she's capable of communicating with animals and their owners at a distance and can conduct sessions over the telephone.

Terri Jay is a pet psychic, energy healer, grief counselor, and horse whisperer.

Jay says she can feel the pet through her owner. It's a connection that she's often able to establish extremely quickly. "By connecting to the pet through the owner, I can find the source of illness, pain, emotional distress, and behavior problems," she explains. "When I get on the phone with one of my clients, I undergo a grounding technique. Usually, I only need the pet's name, its breed, and its age in order to start communicating with it."

She adds, "All of this is possible by using the strongest energy in the universe: love. It transcends everything. I've trained with two mentors who are powerful energy healers. They helped me fine-tune my psychic abilities. I go into each session with no ego, no preconceived notions, and no stake in the outcome."

Jay describes communicating with animals as similar to playing a game of psychic charades. "The animal will convey an emotion, taste, image, sound, smell, or feeling. I then have to decipher it." She explains that, like people, all animals communicate differently. She often picks up on a dog's personality as the dog conveys an image or feeling to her. "I consider myself to be a listener and a translator. When someone asks me what to expect from a session, I tell them to have no expectations or preconceived notions. If they wish to have specific questions for their pet prepared, that's fine. I often get called upon if a dog begins to exhibit sudden behavioral changes that its owner doesn't understand, or if the dog becomes extremely ill and the owner must decide whether or not to put the dog to sleep. Sometimes pet owners will ask more general questions, like, 'Is my dog happy overall?' or 'What activity or food does my dog like best?'" she says.

"When a dog is having behavior problems, I can often discover the root cause of the problem, which the owner can then address," she adds. During the years that Jay has been communicating with dogs, she's found that the most common mistake owners make is not paying attention to the specific breed attributes of the dog they've adopted. For example, a dog might have been bred to be an energetic hunting or working dog, but the owner expects her to be a quiet homebody. "This leads to both the dog and the owner becoming extremely frustrated. If you adopt a dog who is bred to be extremely active, the dog will get bored quickly being locked up in an apartment. That can lead to behavioral and emotional problems. There are a lot of constructive activities, like agility training, that dogs can get involved with to help them burn off energy and use their minds," Jay says.

"One of the most common complaints I hear from dogs of all breeds is that they don't like being patted on the head. They love being stroked, but the dogs hate being hit on the head. Dogs like to be scratched, massaged, and rubbed," she adds.

The first time you work with a pet psychic, you'll probably want to have specific questions prepared. But it's important to maintain an open mind and allow the process to unfold. "Be open to whatever information comes through," Jay advises. "Most people don't truly understand how dogs think and feel, plus they don't initially understand how the process works."

Jay says communicating with animals as a psychic is different from energy healing techniques such as Reiki. She says she can help pinpoint medical problems, but she does not diagnose or prescribe treatments. If a dog has a medical problem, Jay strongly recommends consulting with a veterinarian, although she's also an avid supporter of holistic medicine.

Pet psychics do not require any type of state or federal license or training. The best way to find someone to work with is through a referral or by reading about a psychic in a newspaper or magazine article, and then contacting that person.

"Watch out for psychics who make promises they can't keep or promise you a specific outcome based on how much you're willing to pay," Jay warns. "Some pet psychics charge exorbitant amounts of money. I have found that what a psychic charges has little bearing on their actual ability. A legitimate pet psychic should cost somewhere around $100 or less for a one-hour reading."

Some so-called psychics try to take advantage of or mislead their clients. "If a psychic tells you there's a medical problem with your pet but that you don't need to see a veterinarian, beware of that psychic! When there's a medical issue involved, a good psychic will work hand-in-hand with your veterinarian and people who practice holistic medicine. A charlatan will tell you something scary during the reading and try to charge you a lot of money to fix the problem. For example, they'll say something like your dog has a curse on her, but they can fix it for $500. A psychic should never inspire fear. They should work purely out of love. The psychic should never try to control you or sell you something. Find someone who instills confidence."

11

Bathing and Grooming

Canine Coiffure Keeps Your Dog Looking His Best

There are several reasons why it's a good idea to regularly bathe and groom your dog, paying attention not just to his hair but to his nails, teeth, ears, eyes, and other areas that require special attention. First, there are very definite health benefits. For example, keeping your dog's teeth and gums clean could prolong his life, plus it prevents bad breath. Second, a dog can't be pampered if he's not well groomed, and pampering is what this book is all about.

Whether you choose to handle all the bathing and grooming yourself, make weekly appointments with a professional groomer, or bring your dog to a groomer once a month for a trim but bathe him yourself is entirely up to you.

Bathing Your Own Dog

Bathing your dog can be a wonderful bonding experience for you both. It can also be an activity your dog looks forward to, especially if he enjoys the water. When choosing shampoo and related products, focus not just on the "benefits" the products advertise, but on the ingredients used to make them. Stay away from harsh chemicals, dyes, perfumes, and other additives that, over the long term, aren't good for your dog's hair, skin, or overall health.

The Ingredients in the Shampoo Do Matter

There are plenty of shampoos made just for dogs, just as there are many different brands of shampoos and conditioners for humans. For puppies, many veterinarians recommend using a mild or gentle shampoo, such as Johnson's Baby Shampoo. (Yup, the same stuff you'd use on an infant.) There's a reason why most groomers, breeders, and veterinarians recommend using either baby shampoo or shampoo especially formulated for dogs instead of using shampoo for people. Shampoos made for humans, no matter how mild they claim to be, will typically strip all of the natural oils from a dog's coat, resulting in dryness and flaking. In addition, many people shampoos contain chemicals and perfumes that could be harmful to your dog, especially if they get in his eyes or are ingested.

It's important to understand that the cost of a premium dog shampoo doesn't necessarily translate into quality. Just as with shampoos for people, consumers often pay a premium for a name brand. When it comes to shopping for doggy shampoo and other grooming products, focus on the ingredients more than the brand name.

Tip If you have a young puppy, consult with your veterinarian before bathing him at all. When it's appropriate to begin these activities will vary, based on your dog's breed, size, the climate, and your veterinarian's own beliefs.

Look for a shampoo with all-natural ingredients. Mellow Mutts Dog Shampoo (800-830-1762; www.mellowmutts.com), for example, is a premium-quality line of products that uses only natural ingredients, including floral infusions, vitamins, minerals, and essential oils. It leaves the dog's coat soft, manageable, and smelling wonderful. The products are available online and from upscale pet supply boutiques nationwide.

The company's president, Merna Russell, says, "As we created the product line, we focused on what ingredients we could use that would do the most good for the animals, yet remain affordable. Our products contain no chemicals. We use pure essential oils. We're very particular and use only ingredients that dogs will be able to tolerate. Our products look good, smell good, and feel good to the animal, as well as to their owners."

Don't let the humorous names of the shampoos and products in the Mellow Mutts product line fool you. For example, there's Bruno's Stinky Butts Shampoo and Bruno's Stinky Butts Spritz, which are made for male dogs, and Matilda's Prissy Pooch Shampoo and the Spritz for female dogs. Underneath the humor, though, are serious ingredients. These include natural liquid glycerin soap, purified water, flower water, olive oil, vitamin E, vitamin C, aloe vera, and pure orange, ginger, lemongrass, lime, and eucalyptus essential oils. Glycerin is a humectant, so it attracts moisture to skin. It's a moisturizing ingredient that's been used in the soap-making process since the 1800s. And the essential oils enable you to soothe, pamper, and care for your dog with aromatherapy as you're bathing him.

"Our shampoos care for the dog's hair or fur, but they're also really good for the dog's undercoat and skin," says Russell, who works closely with an on-staff aroma therapist and a homeopathic animal care specialist in developing every product her company sells.

When choosing a shampoo, Russell says you don't need to consider the breed of your dog or the length or thickness of his hair. "If you use an all-natural product, you can shampoo your dog two or three times a week without fear of harming his coat. I recommend bathing a dog once a week. When using most good shampoo products, you can clean an entire dog using only a teaspoon of shampoo and plenty of water. It's important to make sure you rinse off the dog well, so there's no soap residue remaining."

Additional products you might consider at bath time, depending on the length and thickness of your dog's hair, include a conditioner and a detangler. Some type of flea and tick deterrent may also be a good idea, depending on where you live and what time of year it is. This can be in the form of an all-natural spray or an additive to the shampoo, or a stand-alone product that uses chemicals to be effective. Talk to your veterinarian about choosing an effective flea and tick deterrent for your dog.

Russell has also developed a line of spritz products that you simply spray onto your dog while brushing him to remove odors and maintain his freshly groomed appearance between baths or visits to the groomer.

Controlling the Water

Once you've selected your dog's shampoo, you'll need to decide where to actually bathe your dog: your kitchen sink, laundry room sink, shower, bathtub, or outside using a garden hose—but only when the weather is warm. (When it's cool out, never bathe your dog outdoors. You're better off taking him to a groomer or an indoor "do-it-yourself" dog washing facility. Between the cold weather and the cold water from the garden hose, your dog could become ill, plus the experience will be extremely unpleasant for him.) The decision will be greatly narrowed down if you have a medium or large dog who won't fit in a sink.

To make the bathing process faster and easier, consider investing in a professional spray valve that attaches to a standard sink faucet, showerhead, or garden hose, and has a controllable spray and a tangle-free hose. The Professional Spray Valve with 9-Foot Coiled Hose, available from PetEdge (800-738-3343; www.petedge.com), is $89.99 and has attachments that make it possible to hook it up to just about any type of faucet.

The coiled design of the hose on this Professional Sprayer Valve lets you bathe and rinse your pet without struggling with hoses that tangle or get in your way. The heavy-duty, polyurethane hose stretches with your movements and then neatly recoils for easy storage. The sprayer valve is made of lightweight, quality aluminum and has a soft, comfortable rubber grip and a plastic sprayer head. The valve has one-handed spray control with a hold-down clip to reduce hand fatigue. Products similar to the Professional Spray Valve with 9-Foot Coiled Hose are available from pet supply stores nationwide.

A Terry Cloth Bathrobe

To give your pampered pooch the ultimate home day spa treatment, after his bath consider wrapping him in an ultrasoft, absorbent, warm terry cloth robe that's embroidered with his name or initials.

Harry Barker Pets' (800-444-2779; www.harrybarker.com) bathrobe for dogs is made from cotton terry cloth. It has a Velcro closure at the chest and ties behind the back. The robe is available in extra-small (10 to 13 inches long, from neck to tail), small (14 to 17 inches), medium (18 to 22 inches), and large (23 to 29 inches), and in pink, red, or light blue. Matching towels are available. The robes are priced between $20 and $30, depending on the size.

Roxy Hunt Couture (877-476-9948; www.roxyhuntcouture.com) has an adorable terry cloth hoodie for $44.99 that comes in three pastel colors—pink, yellow, and blue—and is available in four sizes. There's also a matching terry duffle bag and towel.

Calvin's Closet Pet Boutique (727-791-2229; www.calvinscloset.com/pureluxury.html) sells $20 doggy robes made from a special cloth that absorbs seven times its weight in water.

Fine Linens for Your Pet

"After the bathing process, you should definitely towel dry your dog," says Russell. "Then, if he won't get too scared and he has long hair, you can use a hair dryer while brushing his coat to finish the drying process. The bathing process should end with you brushing and detangling your dog's hair."

Although many people consider their dog to be a member of the family, they draw the line at sharing a towel with him. If you plan to bathe your own dog, stop by any bath and linen store and buy a selection of plush Egyptian, Turkish, or Brazilian cotton towels for your pampered pooch. Choose towels that have a soft, thick, velvety feel, that are absorbent, and that are large enough for your dog. Plan on spending anywhere from $30 to $50 per bath towel for the highest quality.

When washing your dog's bath towel, use a mild detergent and avoid fabric softener.

So you don't confuse your own towels with your dog's, consider buying monogrammed towels. What dog wouldn't feel pampered being towel-dried in a plush cotton towel embroidered with his name on it?

Gracious Style Fine Linens (888-828-7170; www.graciousstyle.com) is one of many companies that sell premium-quality bath towels for people (which, of course, can also be used on your pampered pooch). The company has a monogramming service. Another company that sells upscale, fine French bath linens is Yves Delorme (800-322-3911; www.yvesdelorme.com).

Grooming Basics

Like coiffure for people, dog grooming is both a skill and an art. It does depend on the breed of dog and the length of his hair, but often for the best, most professional results, you'll want to use a professional groomer to cut and style your dog's hair. However, just like your own hair cut, your dog may need a trip to the pro just once a month. Between visits to the doggy salon, there are a variety of things you can (and should) do, such as brushing your dog's hair, to keep him well groomed and healthy.

Brushing your dog regularly is particularly important if he sheds a lot or has long hair that will easily become tangled and matted. Brushing your dog can be a wonderful bonding experience between you and your pampered pooch, because once you get him to relax, the brushing itself will feel like a massage.

To choose the appropriate type of grooming brush for your dog, ask his professional groomer for advice. The type of brush that's best for your dog's coat will be based on a variety of factors, including the length and thickness of your dog's hair.

> *Tip* You can buy grooming tools at any pet supply store. To save money on name-brand grooming products, contact Pet Edge (800-738-3343; www.petedge.com).

What Happens at the Salon?

Depending on the size of your dog, a basic grooming session, including a bath and a haircut, will cost anywhere from $25 to $50. In addition to bathing your dog and cutting, then styling, his hair, a full-service groomer will often offer a variety of services, usually for an extra fee, including:

+ Canine massage

+ Ear cleaning

+ Flea and tick baths

+ Hand brushing

+ Nail trimming, grinding, and polishing

+ Teeth brushing

+ Various skin moisturizing and coat treatments

Finding a Skilled Groomer

There are many things to consider when choosing a groomer. After all, this is someone you'll be trusting to take charge of your dog while you're not there, and to shape his appearance. The best way to find a groomer is through a referral from a happy customer, your veterinarian, or a respected breeder. If possible, take a look at "before" and "after" photos of clients. When you take an initial tour and meet the groomer, also look at the dogs leaving the grooming facility. Do they look relaxed and fabulous, or scrubbed and stressed?

Tip Too busy to take your dog to a groomer? Some professional groomers have a mobile full-service grooming facility in a van, and will come to you. Others have pick-up and drop-off chauffeur service.

To make the grooming experience more fun for your dog, consider finding a location that also offers supervised doggy daycare. This way, your dog can frolic with a few canine pals for a few hours.

Before using any grooming salon for the first time, make a point to meet the person who will actually be working on your dog. See how that person interacts with your dog and make sure you're both comfortable. If you're not comfortable, seek out another groomer.

Once you find a reliable and skilled groomer, you'll be able to build a long-term relationship, just as you would with your own hairstylist. Here are a few other things that are definitely worth considering when choosing a groomer to work with.

- ✦ What training and qualifications does the groomer have? Some states require a groomer to be licensed and/or certified. Also ask if the groomer is a member in good standing of a professional organization.

- ✦ Does the groomer have experience working with your dog's breed?

- ✦ Is the grooming facility neat and clean?

- ✦ What type of restraint(s) will be used on your dog during the grooming process? Ask specifically how the groomer handles working with a scared, aggressive, or overly frisky dog. Avoid a groomer who uses any type of drug to tranquilize your dog.

- ✦ What brand of shampoos and products will be used on your dog and what ingredients do they contain?

- ✦ What extra services does the groomer offer?

- ✦ How well does the groomer handle and interact with their canine clients?

- ✦ How easy and convenient is it to make an appointment with the groomer?

- ✦ Before your dog's first appointment, the groomer should request basic health information about your dog and should get all your contact information, including your vet's name and an emergency contact.

- ✦ The groomer should ask you questions about the type of haircut or style you want for your dog and should follow your instructions.

Dental Hygiene

Just like people, over time your dog's teeth will build up tartar, which could lead to tooth deterioration, infection, gum disease, bad breath, and even tooth loss. This can be dangerous to your dog's health and well-being. It's your job to help your dog prevent these problems.

In addition to giving your dog special bones and biscuits designed to enhance his dental health and clean his teeth, you'll want to periodically have your dog's teeth brushed and cleaned.

A professional groomer can brush your dog's teeth or you can buy special toothpaste and a doggy toothbrush to do this yourself. Only use toothpaste formulated for dogs when brushing your dog's teeth. The fluoride in our toothpaste is not good for dogs, and they can't rinse and spit, the way we can. Four Paws Pet Dental Toothpaste for Dogs, for example, is available from pet supply superstores nationwide. It comes in a variety of flavors and is less than $6 for a 2.5-ounce tube.

Ideally, you want to brush your dog's teeth at least two to four times a month, plus give him bones or chew toys designed specifically to promote oral hygiene, such as Greenies or Nylabone Nutri Dents (see chapter 2).

Based on your veterinarian's advice, you'll also want to have your dog's teeth professionally cleaned periodically. This must be done by your dog's veterinarian, who will use tools to clean your dog's teeth and gums that are very similar to those of your dentist. Because your dog must be put under anesthesia for this treatment, the cost will be anywhere from $100 to $250, not including pre-operative tests, which can add another $100 or more to the bill. Contact your veterinarian for details about what's involved and how often this treatment is necessary for your dog.

To learn more about your dog's dental health, visit these web sites:

Dental Problems Can Be Painful!

Feeding your dog a lot of table scraps instead of a well-balanced, premium dog food will cause tartar to build up faster, which can lead to gum disease.

Signs of gum disease include bad breath, red and swollen gums, a yellow-brown crust of tartar around the gum line, and pain or bleeding when you touch your dog's gums or mouth. If you notice any of these problems, consult with your veterinarian and have your dog examined promptly.

- ✦ American Veterinary Dental Society: www.avds-online.org

- ✦ American Veterinary Medical Association: www.avma.org

- ✦ Pet Dental: www.petdental.com

- ✦ Veterinary Oral Health Council: www.vohc.org

Trimming Your Dog's Nails

Like people, a dog's nails will keep growing until they're cut. Trimming your dog's nails, at least once a month, is important to your dog's overall health and well-being. Overgrown nails can cause the dog's foot to splay, which can create other structural problems. Well-trimmed nails will also protect you from accidentally getting scratched and will help prevent damage to your furniture and carpeting. Clipping your dog's nails is a simple, painless process that requires the use of an inexpensive guillotine-style dog nail trimmer (available from pet supply stores) or a small pair of nail scissors. Any professional groomer or your veterinarian can also clip your dog's nails. The cost of this service is usually under $10.

Tip PetCo and PetSmart locations that offer grooming services will trim your dog's nails, without an appointment, for $8. The process takes about five minutes (assuming your dog cooperates).

If you choose to trim your dog's nails yourself, make sure a professional groomer or veterinarian shows you how, using the clipper you have bought from your favorite pet supply store. Most dogs do not enjoy having their nails trimmed, and the key here is to start young. From the time your dog is a puppy, as you pet him and rub his belly, also handle and massage his paws. If you build up his comfort level at having his paws touched, trimming his nails will become that much easier.

It's important to avoid trimming each nail too short. Running down the center of each nail there is a bundle of nerves and blood vessels, called the quick. If you accidentally cut into the quick, it will hurt your dog and the nail will bleed. If that happens, apply a coagulant (a pinch of cornstarch will also do) and disinfectant to the nail to stop the bleeding.

For additional information about trimming your dog's nails, visit the Washington State University College of Veterinary Medicine web site at www.vetmed.wsu.edu/cliented/dog_nails.asp.

Polish Perfect

If you decide to polish your dog's nails, never use nail polish or nail polish remover designed for humans. Nail products for humans contain poisonous chemicals that your dog should not inhale or ingest. Instead, buy an epoxy enamel made specifically for dogs. The Pawlish line of doggy nail polish, for example, is available online for $7.95 per bottle from www.ballbeauty.com/opi_pawlish.htm. It comes in a variety of colors. Any professional groomer will also have a selection of safe nail polish that dries quickly.

12

Training, Doggy Daycare, and Resorts

A Trained and Entertained Dog Is a Happy Dog

One of the keys to developing a positive, strong, happy long-term relationship with your dog is to train her as early in her life as possible. A trained dog is a joy to be with. You can take her just about anywhere, and people will welcome her with delight. An untrained dog, on the other hand, doesn't know how to behave in many situations and will therefore do what seems most logical to a dog—which may include pulling, scratching, jumping, barking, and urinating. Train your dog and, when she is unsure, she will look to you for cues about how to behave. You'll both experience less stress and enjoy being together.

One misconception about training is that you take your dog to a bunch of classes, then at the end she graduates as a disciplined and well-mannered member of your family and you never have to do any training again. No matter how good the trainer is, though, training is ongoing. You must take an extremely active role in your dog's education. This means working with her every single day—and not just during the classes, but throughout the day. The purpose of a dog-training class is to teach you how to be the trainer.

As the training process begins, plan on spending from thirty to sixty minutes per day (or longer) working with your dog at home, in addition to taking classes, to teach her basic commands, such as "sit," "stay," "come," and "down." Participating in several ten- to fifteen-minute training sessions throughout the day will work best.

You'll also want to work with your dog, perhaps under the supervision of a professional trainer, to overcome bad habits, such as chewing furniture or excessive barking. Housetraining is also something a professional dog trainer can help you with, but you can also learn how to do it yourself by reading dog training books or watching training DVDs.

Once your dog is properly trained, keeping her entertained is one of your many responsibilities as a pet owner. Socialization with other people and dogs is absolutely necessary if you want a dog who is well adjusted and well trained, and many dogs thrive on it. If, however, you work a full-time job, travel a lot, and have a generally busy life, you won't always have a lot of time to spend with your dog, doing the things she loves to do. To help socialize your dog and ensure she won't be stuck home alone all day, day after day, there are a wide range of doggy daycare centers and resorts that offer supervised play time and exercise for your dog.

Training Options for a Well-Mannered Pooch

Training your dog should begin the very first day you bring her home. If you've never trained a dog before, the concept may seem relatively simple. But if you take the wrong approach, your efforts, no matter how sincere, probably won't generate the desired results; plus, you could scare or confuse your dog.

Many professional trainers will tell you that you must learn how your dog views the world to truly understand her behaviors, then become what she considers to be a benevolent leader. Unfortunately, the desire to spoil her rotten needs to take a backseat when you're trying to train her. As a responsible dog owner, you'll need to learn how to say no to your dog, so she'll understand exactly what you want her to do and what you don't want her to do.

When it comes to dog training, you have a variety of options.

✦ Read dog training books and/or watch training DVDs and do the training yourself. Make sure the training books you read or the videos you watch have advice from highly experienced and well-qualified trainers.

✦ Attend group dog-training classes.

✦ Hire a private dog trainer to come to your home to work with both you and your dog. This can be supplemented with private training sessions between just the trainer and your dog.

Whichever training option you choose, you must also decide on what training approach you'll take. Most trainers and dog owners these days prefer to pursue a positive approach to training. This means you'll concentrate on rewarding her for what she does right, rather than hitting, threatening, yelling, shaking, jerking, or scaring your dog into submission when she does something wrong. Yes, you'll still have to let her know when

Tip Clicker training is one approach to positive training. To learn more about it, point your web browser to www.clickertraining.com.

she has made the wrong choice—because how will she learn if you don't?—but you'll do so gently and without a lot of fuss. Instead, you'll focus on rewards, using endless affection, praise, toys, and treats to help her learn.

Group Training Classes

Dog-training classes are offered throughout the country. They typically meet once a week for between six and eight weeks, and focus on beginner, intermediary, or advanced training topics. By participating in group classes, not only will you learn how to properly train your dog, you'll also have an opportunity to socialize her in a supervised environment. One-hour group training classes cost anywhere from $20 to $50 each.

When choosing a dog-training class, focus first on the training approach that's being taught, then make sure the instructor is qualified and is someone you and your dog will be able to learn from. Consider the number of dogs (and owners) in the class and how much personalized attention you'll receive. Finally, make sure you'll be placed in a class that's appropriate for your dog in terms of the class level, and the age and size of your dog. If you have a small-size puppy, ideally you want to start in a beginner (aka puppy kindergarten) class composed of a small group of other young, small dogs (and their owners).

Pet supply superstores, such as PetCo or PetSmart, typically run dog training or dog obedience classes in their stores. Check these classes out carefully, because some are run by experienced trainers and some are not. There are also many independent schools located throughout the country. Ask for a referral from your veterinarian, groomer, or other dog owners in your area.

Working with a Private Trainer

Private dog training can be expensive, but the benefit is that the instructor works one-on-one with you and your dog, at your convenience. Although your dog won't get the benefit of social interaction with other dogs, the training process could go a bit faster, plus you'll be able to address specific issues you and your dog are facing. For a private trainer, plan on spending anywhere from $35 to $100 per hour, depending on the trainer's qualifications, experience, and reputation.

Just Whisper

The Dog Whisperer, a book by Paul Owens (Adams Media, $10.95), is an excellent training resource for all dog owners, regardless of whether you choose to train your own dog, take classes, or hire a private trainer. Owens has also made a DVD, *The Dog Whisperer: Beginning and Intermediate Dog Training* ($29.95), which can be ordered by calling (800) 955-5440 or visiting his web site at www.dogwhispererdvd.com. Like many trainers today, Owens focuses on a compassionate and positive training approach.

Definitely seek out someone who is well qualified, bonded, and experienced working with your dog's breed. When dealing with certain types of behavior problems, such as biting, snapping, and possessiveness of toys, breed knowledge is essential. You should feel comfortable with the trainer's philosophy and approach. During the training process, your dog should never be harmed, abused, or scared into submission.

Choosing the right private trainer to work with you and your dog from among all the qualified individuals is a matter of personal preference. The trainer's personality and how he or she works with your dog will play a vital role in achieving the objectives you're seeking.

To help find a suitable private trainer, ask for a referral from your veterinarian, groomer, local humane society, or a local dog club. You can also contact the International Association of Canine Professionals (www.dogpro.org) or the Association of Pet Dog Trainers (www.apdt.com). However, never assume that a dog trainer's membership in an association qualifies that person to be a suitable instructor for your dog. Keep in mind that no state or federal agency regulates or licenses dog trainers. It's important for you to investigate the trainer's qualifications before allowing him or her to work with you and your dog. Ask questions, such as how many years of experience they have, what type of education they've received and from where, and, most importantly, what training methods they use. Ask for references from clients, and call those references.

Doggy Daycare: Pampering Even When You're Not Around

Dogs are social creatures and enjoy interacting with people and other dogs. If you have a busy work schedule or find that you must often leave your dog home alone for extended periods of time, seriously consider sending your pampered pooch to doggy daycare. Doggy daycare is designed to provide a fun, social, and safe environment for your dog while you're at work.

Doggy daycare provides supervised activities, human interaction, and social interaction with other dogs. Your dog can play, exercise, and socialize, instead of being cooped up alone at home. This is good for your dog's physical and emotional well-being.

An upscale doggy daycare facility is very different from a traditional kennel that keeps your dog in a cage and provides minimal interaction with humans or other dogs. A doggy daycare center is staffed by qualified and experienced dog care experts, and is equipped with plenty of indoor and outdoor activities and toys for your dog to play with.

The Red Dog Inn & Resort (508-339-5912; www.reddoginnandresort.com), in West Mansfield, Massachusetts, is one example of a center that provides its doggy daycare clients with a wide range of fun and healthy activities. Its facilities include two swimming pools, an outdoor canopied picnic and play area, a lounging area, an outdoor running area, tunnels to explore, piles of dirt to dig in, plenty of supervised interaction with other dogs and people, and an ultraclean indoor play and kennel area where the temperature is maintained at 70 degrees year-round. The indoor area has an ozone air-freshening system that keeps the air clean and fresh. The Red Dog Inn is one of many upscale facilities that also offer full-grooming services, private training, and pet massage as optional services. Meals are provided throughout the day, based on your dog's dietary needs.

Many daycare facilities have half-day or full-day rates. You're responsible for dropping off and picking up your dog at prearranged times, so try to find a facility that's close to home or is on your way to work.

Before you drop off your dog at a daycare facility, do your research, interview the people running the facility, and take a tour. You obviously want the people running the daycare center and supervising your dog's play to be well qualified, skilled at working with animals, and extremely responsible and caring. You also want to find a facility that's reputable, clean, odor-free, and that will never tranquilize or medicate your dog or lock your dog in a small cage or crate (although crating in a roomy, comfortable crate may occasionally be necessary).

Tip Some upscale doggy daycare facilities are equipped with web cams, so clients can log onto the Internet and see live video of their dog at play. If the daycare facility you choose doesn't offer this, consider making occasional surprise visits to check on your dog when you first start with a new daycare service.

A reputable doggy daycare facility will require all dogs to be up-to-date on all of their vaccinations and be using some type of flea and tick preventive. The facility will also evaluate each dog carefully to be sure she'll interact safely with other dogs before admitting her into the daycare program. Many facilities will also require all dogs to be spayed or neutered and housetrained.

The best way to find a doggy daycare facility in your area is to ask for a referral from your veterinarian, groomer, local dog club or human society, or fellow dog owners. Plan on spending anywhere from $20 to $35 per day (six to eight hours) for doggy daycare services. Many facilities offer discounts when you prepay for a week or a block of days in advance.

Professional Dog Walkers

A professional dog walker is someone who loves dogs and will come to your home once or twice a day to walk your dog while you're at work. This is typically someone from your community who operates their own business and who is insured, bonded, and certified. Most professional dog walkers have some training and know how to properly handle animals, and they're familiar with emergency first aid techniques for dogs.

In addition to being able to handle your dog well, the person you hire must be trustworthy and reliable, since you'll need to give the dog walker a key to your home and rely on them to show up when they're supposed to. Your dog will be able to remain in a familiar environment, yet receive social interaction and exercise while you're out.

Tip To find a professional dog walker, visit the Puppy Walkers web site (www.puppywalkers.com).

Most dog walkers will spend between fifteen and thirty minutes of one-on-one time with your dog and charge anywhere from $10 to $25 per visit. Your best bet for finding a reliable, professional dog walker is to pay attention to someone you see day after day walking dogs in your community and ask for their business card. If you need referrals for a dog walker, you can also ask your veterinarian, your groomer, and your neighbors.

Before hiring someone, have them come to your home for a consultation and watch as they spend time interacting with your dog. Make sure you feel totally comfortable leaving your dog in that person's care. Also ask the dog walker for their credentials and references, and then call those references.

When interviewing a dog walker, ask how many dogs they usually walk at one time. Some dogs enjoy the social interaction of walking and exercising with other dogs. Others don't get along with other dogs and prefer one-on-one human interaction from the person walking them. The decision about whether to allow your dog to be walked with others should be based on your dog's preference and safety. If your dog will be walked with other dogs, make sure the other dogs are approximately the same size as your dog and are all trained. Unpredictable behavior from one dog could be dangerous for all the dogs. Remember, most dog walkers are *not* professional trainers.

Make sure the dog walker doesn't use a choke collar or any other type of collar that could injure your dog. Also find out if the dog walker will feed your dog or administer medications, if necessary. If you're paying for the dog walker to give your dog one-on-one attention while you're away, you don't want that person talking on their cell phone or sitting on a bench while the dog walks around on an extending leash. If the dog walker has a bunch of clients in your neighborhood, you should be able to spot them on the job and evaluate the interaction they give to their canine clients before leaving your dog in their care.

One of the challenges of hiring a professional dog walker will be finding someone in your community who can work around your schedule. You'll need to decide if you want the dog walker to visit once or twice a day and which days of the week. Make sure you all agree on time(s) the dog walker should visit, and find out how flexible their schedule is. Find out if they can accommodate last-minute changes, too. Having someone on call to care for your dog while you're at work or if you have to unexpectedly work late will provide you with piece of mind, knowing that your dog is properly cared for.

Upscale Canine Resorts

If you're traveling and can't take your dog with you, you may need to find a place to board your dog. Leaving your dog overnight—whether it's in your home with a dog walker coming to visit, at home with a dog sitter staying with her, or dropping her at a boarding facility or resort—is never an easy thing to do. To make the process easier on both you and your dog, do your research in advance to find the best possible options and be willing to pay for the best services possible. When you ultimately leave your dog, it's important to know that she is being properly cared for, fed, supervised, and, of course, pampered.

Most run-of-the-mill kennels will lock your dog in a pen, offering her little time for exercise and personal attention. An alternative is to find an upscale dog resort in your area. A dog resort, as the name suggests, pampers your dog and has first-class accommodations. Many dog resorts have private suites (rooms, not cages or pens) equipped with a couch, television, and plenty of space to run around and play with her favorite toys. Some even have fenced outdoor decks, enabling your dog to roam freely outside or stay inside when she's not engaged in supervised play or other organized activities.

Dog resorts also have a wide range of services, some of which are included in the overnight fee and some of which cost extra. For example, some dog resorts have one-on-one supervised playtime, supervised group playtime with other dogs, dog grooming services, pet massage, and a full menu of specially prepared meals and gourmet treats.

A VIP suite at an upscale dog resort will cost more than $50 per night (plus extras). However, you can be sure your dog will be pampered and receive plenty of personal attention.

Look for Certification

The facility where you board your dog should be a member in good standing of the American Boarding Kennels Association (www.abka.com). According to the ABKA web site, "The Voluntary Facilities Accreditation (VFA) Program is a professional program, which requires participating boarding kennels to demonstrate their adherence to a comprehensive set of operational standards. These standards include more than two hundred detailed requirements for boarding kennels and were developed over many years by the ABKA, the international trade association for the owners and operators of commercial boarding kennels. The standards reflect the views of kennel operators, veterinarians, pet owners, and humane organizations, and thus represent the 'state of the art' in animal care and management."

Another way to check up on the reputation of a doggy daycare facility, dog walker, or dog resort in your area is to contact your local Better Business Bureau (www.bbb.org).

Dog-Sitting Services: An Alternative to Boarding

If you'll be away for one or more nights, you might not want to send your dog away from home, no matter how nice the local canine resort. One option is to hire a professional pet sitter to take care of your dog while you're away. Some pet sitters make several stops a day at your home (you specify how many, and pay for each), and some will live in your home while you're away, giving your dog nonstop, one-on-one attention.

When looking for a dog sitter, follow the same general rules as you would for finding a professional dog walker. However, you also want to make sure you can trust the person you hire, not just to care for your dog, but to be alone in your home. The pet sitter should be insured and bonded and come highly recommended by a friend, coworker, veterinarian, groomer, or someone else you trust. Always ask the pet sitter for references, and check them carefully.

Most pet sitters will also handle other household chores while you're away, such as watering plants and bringing in the mail. The cost will vary dramatically, based on where you live, the experience of the pet sitter, and what services are offered. With more than 27,000 members, Pet Sitters International (336-983-9222; www.petsit.com) is an excellent online resource for learning about pet-sitting services. The organization has four levels of accreditation for professional pet sitters and provides dog owners with valuable information and a free online referral service.

The very best dog resorts are operated by dog lovers who are specially trained to handle dogs. You find the best possible dog resort or boarding facility much the same way you'd find the best doggy daycare facility. Do your research, ask for referrals, tour the facility, and, during your tour, ask lots of questions. Make sure the facility is clean and sanitary, but also make sure your dog won't be directly exposed to any harmful cleaning or sanitizing chemicals. Also, the boarding facility should require, with no exceptions, that all dogs be up-to-date on their vaccinations and be using some type of flea and tick preventive. Make sure the dog resort or boarding facility will give your dog the brand of food she is used to and will keep her on the same dining schedule.

If you tour a boarding facility and find a lot of dirty cages or play areas, smell strong odors, notice poor ventilation, come across seemingly unhappy dogs, or spot generally unhealthy conditions, find another facility! Also, pay careful attention to how well the facility's workers interact with the dogs. Remember, your dog is relying on you to find the best possible facility to ensure a safe, nonstressful, happy, and healthy stay when she has to be away from home.

Before dropping off your dog, make sure you understand what services will be offered and what the rates for those services will be. Before leaving your dog for an overnight stay, consider using the facility for doggy daycare for several afternoons to see how things work out and how your dog reacts. Understand that being away from home and in an unfamiliar environment can be extremely stressful for your dog. Work with the dog resort to make sure this stress is minimized as much as possible. In case something goes wrong, determine, in advance, how the facility deals with problems, such as medical emergencies.

People who are in the habit of pampering their pooch tend to reserve overnight boarding as an absolute last resort if they have to travel. For one-night getaways, finding a dog walker to visit your home may be a more suitable option for your dog. Understand, however, that if you find a high-quality dog resort, the experience for your dog will be a safe and pleasurable one. Plus, you can travel knowing your dog is being well cared for in a supervised environment.

Tip To help your dog feel right at home in the new surroundings, be sure to leave her with her favorite blanket and a few of her own toys.

13

Traveling with Your Dog

Bringing Your Pampered Pooch on Vacation

Sure, there are plenty of upscale doggy daycare and overnight boarding facilities where you can leave your dog when you go on a business trip or vacation. Some of these facilities have luxury private suites, specially prepared meals, cable television, supervised group or one-on-one playtime, full grooming services, and even daily massages.

However, some dog owners prefer to take their best friend with them when they travel. This chapter focuses on how to prepare for the trip, safely travel with your dog, and choose appropriate accommodations. With the ever-changing restrictions and regulations imposed by airlines, tourist destinations, and accommodations, traveling with your dog will require extra planning. But it can result in a fun, memorable, and rewarding experience for you and your dog.

Especially if you have a well-trained and reliably housetrained small dog, taking him on a trip probably won't be too difficult or stressful. Medium and large dogs can be more difficult to travel with, especially if you'll be traveling by airplane and/or want to stay at luxury hotels.

When you're thinking about whether to bring your dog along as a travel companion, consider the following:

+ The emotional impact on you and your dog if you leave him behind in a kennel, doggy resort, with friends or relatives, or at home with a dog sitter.

+ Whether bringing your dog with you will put too much stress on you and your dog.

+ The cost of leaving your dog at home. Be sure to calculate the daily cost of boarding or the dog sitter.

♦ The cost of bringing your dog with you on the trip. Be sure to calculate the fees charged by the airlines, hotel, etc., plus any dog-walking or dog-sitting services you'll need while on vacation. In many cases, even bringing a small dog with you on vacation can cost the same as bringing a child.

♦ Your vacation destination. If you're traveling outside the United States or Canada, traveling with your dog can be extremely difficult and expensive—if it's allowed at all. For domestic travel, your destination and how you plan to spend your time should have some impact on your decision about whether to travel with your dog.

The good news for dog owners is that more and more popular vacation destinations are becoming dog friendly. Many hotels and resorts now allow at least smaller dogs in guest rooms, although they often charge an extra fee. If you'll be traveling to your vacation destination by car, as long as your dog doesn't get carsick, planning your trip will be relatively simple. As you're driving, plan on stopping every few hours to give your dog a walk. Beyond that, simply set up a comfortable car seat or safety harness in your vehicle for him (see chapter 8), pack his belongings, and you're ready to go.

> *Tip* If you're planning a vacation and need to leave your dog in an overnight boarding facility or want to have someone come to your house to dog sit or walk your dog, be sure to read chapter 12.

Airplane trips with your dog require extra planning, but are usually also doable, especially with smaller dogs. As you're planning your trip and booking airline reservations, be mindful of the travel restrictions, regulations, and guidelines imposed by the airlines (many of which are outlined later in this chapter but are always subject to change).

Choosing Your Vacation Destination

When choosing a vacation destination, consider the location and the hotel, resort, or rental property where you'll be staying. Are dogs allowed to stay in the guest rooms? Will there be someplace to walk your dog or allow your dog to run around? What will you do with your dog during the day when you're visiting tourist destinations, sightseeing, shopping, and eating? Can you leave your dog unattended in the hotel room? Will you need to hire a local dog walker? Do you plan to leave your dog in a nearby doggy daycare facility while you're sightseeing or spending the day at the beach?

Some popular vacation destinations, including Walt Disney World in Orlando, Florida, and Disneyland in Anaheim, California, have on-site kennels but don't allow dogs to stay in on-property resorts or to visit the various theme parks. Other popular destinations, such as the Las Vegas resorts located along the Strip, are not suitable for pets. Find out what is and isn't possible where you plan to go.

Before booking your travel, figure out what your needs will be and how traveling with your dog will affect your daily vacation itinerary, and make sure the dog-related services you need (dog walking, doggy daycare, grooming, and so on) will be available near where you'll be staying.

Tip Once you decide where you're going on vacation, make sure you plan in advance how your dog will spend his days while you're off sightseeing, shopping, dining, visiting museums, or spending the day at the beach. Many of these places don't allow dogs.

Check with Your Veterinarian *Before* Leaving Home

If you'll be traveling with your dog by airplane or you plan to put him in doggy daycare or a kennel while you're away, before you leave home, consult with your veterinarian and make sure you get a written health certificate. This is a letter, on your veterinarian's letterhead, stating your dog is healthy and is up-to-date on all his vaccinations. You'll also want to get a printed copy of your dog's vaccination records and have these documents with you when you travel.

Some airlines will ask to see this paperwork when you check in at the airport. All doggy daycare facilities, kennels, and grooming facilities will also require you to submit this paperwork. If your dog is up-to-date on his annual veterinary visits, obtaining a health certificate should require little more than a quick phone call to the veterinarian.

If you'll be traveling with your dog on an airplane, consult with your veterinarian about whether it's necessary to sedate him for the journey. Veterinarians have mixed opinions on this, and the American Veterinary Medical Association recommends against it, if at all possible, because sedation at high altitudes can have side effects. Nonetheless, from your dog's standpoint, airline travel can be extremely stressful, especially if he won't be traveling in the cabin with you. Plus, he'll be cooped up in a carrier or crate for the duration of the flight. If you have a very hyperactive or anxious dog, your veterinarian may want to prescribe a sedative for your dog that will help ease the stresses of travel.

Travel Expenses to Consider

Traveling with your dog can get expensive. The following are some of the expenses you might incur; they should be added to your travel budget.

- ✦ **Airline fees:** Most airlines charge between $50 and $100 per flight, each way, to travel with your dog, whether the dog accompanies you in the cabin or you check him as baggage and he travels in the cargo hold.

- ✦ **Hotel fees:** Many hotels that accept dogs have a per-visit pet charge. In some cases this is refundable, but in many cases it's not. Some Ritz-Carlton Hotels in the United States, for example, have a nonrefundable $125 to $175 pet charge, plus they charge for extras, such as room service for your dog and dog walking. For a dog to stay at a Ritz-Carlton, he must weigh less than 50 pounds.

◆ **Veterinary visit:** If you need to have your pet examined to receive a health certificate, a basic exam will cost between $30 and $100, depending on your veterinarian and whether you have pet insurance.

◆ **Dog sitting, daycare, and walking services:** If you plan to leave your dog while you're out sightseeing, chances are you'll want to make arrangements for his care. Whether you drop him off at a local doggy daycare facility or arrange for a dog walker to come to your hotel, the cost will be between $20 and $50 per day.

What to Pack for Your Dog

When on vacation, your dog will need all or most of the comforts he's used to at home. It's a good idea to pack a separate suitcase or carry-on for your dog, so everything he'll need is readily available and organized.

Tip Many taxis, shuttles, and car services do not allow dogs. So, if you'll need ground transportation, you may be forced to rent a car, for example, to get to and from the airport.

Be sure to pack an ample supply of your dog's usual food and treats, plus his favorite toys and other necessities. The following packing list is a good start for your pampered pooch; add or subtract your own items, based on what your dog needs.

◆ Bed and/or blanket

◆ Bottled water

◆ Carrier or crate

◆ Car seat

◆ Chew toys

◆ Clothing

◆ Doggy waste bags

◆ Dog tag that displays your name and cell phone number, in addition to your home phone

- ◆ Flashlight (for walking your dog at night)

- ◆ Food and water bowls

- ◆ Food, canned and dry

- ◆ Grooming brush

- ◆ Health certificate and immunization records

- ◆ Leash and collar/harness

- ◆ Portable pen

- ◆ Prescription medications and/or vitamins

- ◆ Toys

- ◆ Treats

- ◆ Wee-wee pads or newspaper (or other disposable housetraining pads, if your dog is paper trained)

Tip Bring an ample supply of your dog's regular brand of food on the trip. Don't count on the local pet supply stores at your destination to stock the brand you want, especially if you feed your dog a premium brand that's not available in supermarkets. You can store dry food in resealable plastic containers. If your canned dog food doesn't include an easy-open lid, be sure to pack a can opener.

The following products might help you and your pampered pooch better enjoy your vacation.

Outward Hound Pet-Saver Lifejacket

Price: $16 to $35, depending on size
Manufacturer: The Kyjen Company, Inc.
Phone: (800) 477-5735
Web site: www.kyjen.com
Availability: Online and from pet supply stores nationwide

If you'll be taking your dog on a boat, consider investing in a dog life jacket. By law, even people who know how to swim must wear a life jacket while aboard many types of boats. While the law doesn't require that your dog wear one, your desire to protect your pet should. Even pets who know how to swim could be injured falling overboard or become too traumatized to swim, especially in bad weather. A life jacket could save their life in an emergency. Outward Hound's Pet-Saver Lifejacket is a high-performance dog flotation device. It's available in easily seen neon orange and black and is made from a tough, denier nylon, which is soft yet durable. The life jacket fits on a dog like a harness and has a top grab handle for easy rescue by hand or boat hook.

Pet-Saver Lifejackets are available in five fully adjustable sizes to accommodate any size dog.

Even if your dog knows how to swim and is comfortable around water, a Pet-Saver Lifejacket is an important safety device if you'll be boating, fishing, sailing, or participating in water sport adventures.

Home-N-Go Pet Pen

Price: $89.99
Manufacturer: PetEdge
Phone: (800) 738-3343
Web site: www.petedge.com
Availability: Online or from pet supply stores nationwide

Parents of infants often bring a portable crib when traveling. The Home-N-Go Pet Pen is a portable pen for your small dog that does the exact same thing as a crib: keep your dog safe and out of trouble. When set up, the pen measures 36 by 23 by 26 inches; it folds down to a mere 36 by 23 by 4 ½ inches and comes with a carrying case (complete with shoulder strap). It weighs about 15 pounds and can be checked on an airplane as baggage.

The Pet Pen has a sturdy metal frame and a durable blue nylon lining with black mesh sides. The top is open, so you can easily reach in. The floor is padded and has a water-resistant plastic lining. One side of the pen opens fully with a sturdy zipper.

The Pet Pen is great for keeping a small dog safe in a hotel room, for example, especially when he'll be left unattended. Set-up takes about five minutes, once you get the hang of how the safety locks on the frame work.

Dog owners can tote along a convenient Home-N-Go portable pet pen to keep their dog safe and out of trouble.

Doggles Dog Eyewear

Price: $25
Manufacturer: Midknight Creations, LLC
Phone: (866) DOGGLES
Web site: www.doggles.com
Availability: Online or from pet supply stores nationwide

Dogs have certainly been around for thousands, perhaps millions of years and have thrived in the outdoors without the protection of sunglasses. Yet for active dogs and dogs who enjoy being pampered in the sun, Midknight Creations offers a line of designer Doggles—sunglasses for dogs.

"Whenever I hear a dog likes to hang its head out of a car window or ride on a boat across a lake, I recommend protective eyewear for the dog," says Michael Brickman, DVM, a veterinary ophthalmologist at Veterinary Ophthalmology Service in Ontario, Canada (www.eyevet.ca). "Eyewear for dogs is important to protect the animal's delicate eye tissue." Protective eyewear is also sometimes helpful after a dog has cataract surgery.

Doggles have shatterproof, antifog, polycarbonate lenses, which provide 100 percent protection against the UV rays of the sun. They're also designed to protect your dog from wind and debris, while he shows off an ultracool style and hip attitude. The company has a selection of designer frames and interchangeable lenses. They're held on the dog's face with an adjustable elastic strap.

What's next? Well, according to Midknight Creations, it's currently researching prescription eyewear for dogs.

Traveling by Airplane

If you're traveling just within the United States and Canada, having your dog accompany you on an airplane is relatively easy, as long as you're mindful of travel guidelines and limitations. For example, on most flights, no more than three small pets are allowed to travel in the cabin (one pet in first class and two in the coach on most airlines). During peak travel times, these slots book up quickly, so it's important to make your reservations early.

At the time you book your airline tickets, be sure to tell the airline you'll be traveling with a dog and be prepared to pay an extra fee (between $50 and $100 each way, depending on the airline). A pet carrier counts as one carry-on bag, but you still have to pay the fee. In most cases, you'll be given a separate reservation number for your dog. Make sure you get confirmation directly from the airline before the date of your travel. If you book your airline tickets online, especially through a discount service such as Hotwire, Travelocity, Priceline, or Orbitz, you'll still need to book your dog's travel reservations directly with the airline.

Vacationing in a sunny place? Protect your dog's eyes with designer Doggles eyewear.

If the dog weighs less than 15 pounds, is more than 8 weeks old, and is fully weaned, he can accompany you in the cabin and travel under the seat in front of you, as long as he remains inside an airline-approved carrier. (See chapter 8 for details about choosing a carrier for your dog.) Even on long flights, you're not allowed to remove your dog from his carrier while in flight.

Larger dogs will need to be checked as baggage and fly within the plane's pressurized cargo hold within an appropriate hard-bodied crate. At some times of the year, depending on where you're flying to and from, and the size and breed of your dog, most airlines will not allow pets to be checked in the cargo hold as a safety precaution. Some restrict travel during the very warm and very cold months, while others allow or disallow dogs to fly based on the local weather. Contact your airline for details and restrictions, then plan your travel accordingly.

What is approved for in-cabin flight and as checked baggage varies from airline to airline, so be sure to ask when you call to make your pet's reservation. On American Airlines, for example, the maximum size for pet carriers in the cabin is 23 inches long by 13 inches wide by 9 inches high.

Within the carrier, your dog must be able to stand up, turn around, and lie down in a natural position. The maximum size for crates taken along as checked baggage is 40 inches long by 27 inches wide by 30 inches high. However, the maximum size kennel (series 500) is not accepted on Boeing MD-80 aircraft. Series 700 kennels are not allowed on any American Airlines aircraft. The maximum weight of a checked pet and kennel (combined) cannot exceed 100 pounds.

These are the rules for just one airline. To learn more about the specific travel guidelines of popular airlines, contact them directly.

✦ American Airlines: (800) 433-7300; www.aa.com/content/travelInformation/specialAssistance/travelingWithPets.jhtml

✦ Continental Airlines: (800) 575-3335; www.continental.com/travel/policies/animals/default.asp

✦ Delta Air Lines: (800) 221-1212; www.delta.com/planning_reservations/special_travel_needs/pet_travel_information/index.jsp

✦ JetBlue: (800) JET-BLUE; www.jetblue.com/travelinfo/howToDetail.asp?topicId=8

✦ Northwest Airlines: (800) 225-2525; www.nwa.com/travel/animals/index.html

✦ Southwest Airlines: At the time this book was written, the airline's web site said, "Southwest Airlines does not accept live animals in the aircraft cabin or cargo compartment other than fully trained service animals accompanying a person with a disability or being delivered to a person with a disability." You can check for updated information at www.southwest.com.

✦ United Airlines: (800) 864-8331; www.united.com/page/article/0,6722,51255,00.html

Arrive at the airport at least ninety minutes to two hours early on the day of your trip. You can't use curbside check-in or the automated self-service check-in kiosks; you must check in face to face, and the line to check in with an agent is often long. Be prepared to provide your reservation number or airline tickets, your photo identification, and your dog's health certificate. The airline representative may also inspect the dog's carrier or crate and ask to see the dog.

At this point, if the dog will be traveling as checked cargo, he'll be turned over to an airline representative and loaded onto the airplane. You should then proceed to the security checkpoint and head to your appropriate gate.

Hard-Bodied Crates

Petmate (877-738-6283; www.petmate.com) and SkyKennel (distributed by PetEdge, 800-738-3343; www.petedge.com) are two companies that offer airline-approved, hard-bodied crates that can be purchased online or from pet supply stores. The crates are made from heavy-duty, high-impact plastic and come in a variety of sizes.

Many airlines will sell or rent hard-bodied carriers at major airports. Check with your airline for details.

After passing through security, your dog must be placed back in his carrier and kept inside until you reach your destination city and exit the airport. Few airports have places where you can walk your dog once you pass through the security checkpoint, so plan accordingly. Make sure you walk your dog before entering the airport in your departure city. Don't give him any food or water for several hours before a flight. Once you land, however, make sure you give him water, since he could become dehydrated from flying (just as people do). If the dog will be checked as baggage, you will be required to supply food and water within his crate. All the more reason to make sure he gets a long walk and relieves himself before you enter the airport.

Although airport regulations say your dog must remain within his carrier at all times inside the airport, you'll discover that, depending on the airport, there is some leniency regarding this rule. As you're waiting for a flight near your boarding gate, for example, airport security will sometimes look the other way if you take a small dog out of his carrier and hold him for a few minutes.

Once on the airplane, however, the dog must stay within his carrier at all times. You may find it beneficial to take your dog into the airplane's lavatory, put down the baby changing table, remove him from his carrier, and allow him to stretch during a long flight. What you do in the privacy of the locked lavatory is your business, although you and your dog won't have too much space to move around.

Bus or Train . . . No Dogs Allowed!

Amtrak and commercial bus companies such as Greyhound only allow service dogs on their trains and buses. No other pets are permitted. This is also the case on most regional and commuter train and bus services, so plan accordingly. Regulations vary among tour bus companies, so contact the company directly, well in advance, to learn whether dogs are allowed.

Traveling by Car

Whether you're taking a road trip in your own car or your dog will be riding with you in a rental car, be sure to bring a car seat, harness, or restraint device so your dog can travel safely within the vehicle (see chapter 8). If your dog tends to shed, consider covering the car seats with a blanket, especially in a rental car. You don't want to be charged extra for cleaning fees or damage to the vehicle.

As you're driving, allow extra time in your travel schedule to make frequent rest stops to walk and feed your dog. Especially in warm weather, avoid leaving your dog unattended within a vehicle, even for a few minutes. If you absolutely must leave your dog for a few minutes, leave windows open for ventilation (but not open enough for him to escape), plus provide plenty of water in the car. The temperature within your vehicle (even with the windows cracked open) can climb from 75 degrees to more than 95 degrees in just fifteen minutes on a warm day. Don't take chances. Sure, you could leave your dog locked in a crate, somehow chain the crate to your car (so it can't be stolen), then leave all the car's windows wide open, but taking these drastic measures should only be a last resort. Instead of leaving your dog in the car while you dine out in a restaurant, for example, get take-out. Leaving your dog in a hot environment is extremely cruel and very dangerous.

> ### Cars for Dogs . . . and Their Owners
>
> Some car manufacturers, including Honda, have begun designing new cars with dogs in mind. The Honda Wow (Wonderful Open-Hearted Wagon), unveiled at the Tokyo Motor Show in late 2005, has a built-in small dog carrier instead of a glove compartment, and a bigger pop-up travel crate in the backseat. The small SUV also has a removable and washable floor and wide sliding doors. It'll be a dream vehicle for pet owners and pampered pooches, if it is eventually released in the United States.

Finding Dog-Friendly Accommodations

More and more hotels and motel chains, bed-and-breakfasts, inns, rental properties, campgrounds, RV parks, cabins, and other vacation accommodations allow dogs. Not all dogs, though: You're more likely to find accommodations that accept small dogs than medium or large ones.

Around the country, B&B operators who are also dog lovers will often go out of their way to make your pampered pooch feel right at home. Some even have special services that cater to dog owners, such as fenced-in play areas or agreements with local dog-walking or pet-sitting services.

You'll also have more freedom if you go for a short-term rental property, as opposed to a traditional hotel or motel room. The trick, of course, is finding accommodations that meet both your needs and your dog's. This is best done either through a referral from a fellow dog owner or by using one of the dog-friendly travel services described in the section "Working with a Travel Agent" later in this chapter.

Many individual hotels in the following chains are pet-friendly.

+ AmeriSuites: (877) 877-8886

+ Best Western: (800) 780-7234

+ Double Tree Inns: (800) 222-TREE

+ Extended Stay Hotels: (800) 804-3724

+ Hilton: (800) HILTONS

+ Holiday Inn: (888) 890-0242

+ La Quinta Inns & Suites: (866) 725-1661

+ Loews Hotels: (800) 23-LOEWS

+ Red Roof Inns: (800) 733-7663

+ Residence Inns by Marriott: (888) 236-2427

+ Sheraton: (800) 598-1753

+ Travelodge: (800) 578-7878

Be sure to check with each individual location for room availability, since only a limited number of rooms are usually made available to people traveling with pets. And some properties within these chains don't allow pets.

You'll also discover that many upscale hotels, such as the Ritz-Carlton (800-241-3333), the Four Seasons (800-819-5053), and W Hotels (888-625-5144), are mostly pet-friendly, but have specific requirements about the dog's maximum size. Some of these upscale properties also have special services that cater to dogs. At many Ritz-Carlton locations in the United States, for example, the hotel will give your dog his own luxury bed, food and water bowls, and gourmet treats. A special room service menu is also available for dogs, and a dog-walking service is on call (for a fee).

Tip The Hot Deals on Hotels web site (www.hotdealsonhotels.com/pets/sitemap.html) has a free listing of hotels and motels throughout the United States that are dog friendly. From this site, you can also make hotel reservations using a major credit card.

Don't just check in and go! When you arrive at your hotel, spend some time in the room with your dog so he can become acclimated to his surroundings before you leave him alone in the room. If you do leave your dog unattended, always post the "Do Not Disturb" sign on your door. Also, consider placing your dog in an enclosed pet pen or keeping him in the hotel's bathroom so he won't damage the furniture or soil the carpets while you're away. Ideally, you want to take your dog outside when the housekeepers come to make the beds and clean the room.

Working with a Travel Agent

If you'll be using a travel agent to make your arrangements, make sure the agent is knowledgeable and experienced when it comes to pet travel and is up to date on the ever-changing rules, regulations, and extra charges imposed by airlines and hotels. There are a handful of travel agents and services that specialize in traveling with dogs. These companies are familiar with all the latest airline requirements and the best hotels to stay in, and they offer a variety of other services to make traveling with your pet as stress free as possible.

Here are a few of these full-service travel agents, as well as some online services that cater to people traveling with their dog.

Puppy Travel

Phone: (877) 261-3555
Web site: www.puppytravel.com

Puppy Travel is a full-service travel agency for people traveling with their dogs or dogs traveling alone. To help you plan a vacation or business trip with your pet, Puppy Travel will:

✦ Research all airlines, rates, and flight information, based on your desired destination(s)

✦ Prepare a budget for your trip, including all additional pet-related fees charged by the airlines and hotels

✦ Tell you about airline rules and regulations regarding traveling with your pet

✦ Make all travel reservations and bookings for you

✦ Provide information about choosing the right pet carrier or crate for the trip

✦ Answer all travel questions and provide you with useful pretravel checklists

If you need to transport your dog between cities or internationally, unaccompanied, Puppy Travel can also handle all of the logistics and provide door-to-door pick-up and delivery.

Pet Friendly Travel

Web site: www.petfriendlytravel.com

This is an online service that offers an extensive database of pet-friendly hotels and resorts throughout the country. It's an advertiser-supported service that describes accommodations and enables pet owners to search by vacation destination or keyword. The web site also lists dog-friendly beaches throughout the United States and Canada.

Take Your Pet

Phone: (800) 790-5455
Web site: www.takeyourpet.com

This online service offers an abundance of travel information of interest to dog owners, including a directory of pet-friendly accommodations throughout the country. Membership, which is $14.95 a year, is required for access.

The directory has more than 20,000 listings, including bed-and-breakfasts, cabins, hotels, motels, and resorts. Members of this service enjoy up to a 30 percent discount on pet-friendly accommodations at participating hotels and resorts.

To help make the most of your trip, Take Your Pet also has a comprehensive online directory of veterinarians, animal hospitals, shelters, groomers, kennels, boarding facilities, exercise and pet sitting services, and pet food and supply stores. The directory has more than 60,000 listings for companies and services nationwide.

Members also have access to an interactive bulletin board where pet owners can swap advice and travel stories.

Pets on the Go

Phone: (781) 934-7202
Web site: www.petsonthego.com

Pets on the Go is an online service that offers its members informative articles relating to pet travel. You'll also find a comprehensive directory of pet-friendly travel accommodations (with more than 18,000 listings), reviews of accommodations, a team of travel experts who can provide personalized advice and answers to questions online, and a handful of other services.

Access to the web site costs $15 per year. For an annual fee of $30, the membership package also includes a one-year subscription to *Fido Friendly* magazine and a one-year membership to the Help-4-Pets Pet Protection System.

Appendix

Online Resources

For those of you who just can't wait to begin shopping, here is an easy-to-search list of web sites for many of the products and services described in this book.

Food, Water, and Treats

Buddy Biscuit Mix: www.gooddogexpress.com
Doggie Springs: www.doggiesprings.com
Dog Town Bites Premium Dog Biscuits: www.dogtownbites.com
Fortunate Dog Cookies: www.fortunatedogcookies.com
Halo Liv-A-Littles: www.halopets.com
Just Dogs Gourmet Biscuits, Cookies, and Treats: www.justdogsgourmet.com
Merrick: www.merrickpetcare.com
Moo! Free Range Bully Sticks: www.freerangedogchews.com
Natural Choice: www.nutroproducts.com
Prairie: www.naturesvariety.com
Zuke's Mini Naturals: www.zukes.com

Couture

Aurora Sheepskins: www.aurorapetproducts.com
Bark Jacobs: www.barkjacobs.com
Burberry: www.burberry.com
Casual Canine: www.petedge.com
Fifi & Romeo: www.fifiandromeo.com
Friends of Babydoll Collection: www.donaldjpliner.com
The Gilded Paw: www.thegildedpaw.com
Glamourdog: www.glamourdog.com
Gucci: www.gucci.com
Han Nari: www.creativeyoko.co.jp/hannari/top.htm
Happy Paws Pet Clothes: www.happypawsdaycare.com/id14.html
House of Canine Couture: www.caninecouture.ca
Louisdog: www.louisdog.com
Pets at Play: www.petsatplay.com
Polo Ralph Lauren: www.polo.com
Roxy Hunt Couture: www.roxyhuntcouture.com
Scooter's Friends: www.scootersfriends.com
The Toby Line: www.thetobyline.com

Collars, Leashes, and Tags

Bamboo Quick Control Collar: www.bamboopet.com
Bark Avenue Jewelers' Dog Tags and Pendants: www.barkavenuejewelers.com
Bella Paris Harnesses: www.bellaparis.com
Bella Tocca Dog Tags: www.bellatoccatags.com
Cloak & Dawggie Harnesses: www.cloakanddawggie.com
Coach Collars and Leashes: www.coach.com
Earth Dog Collars and Leashes: www.earthdog.com
FlexiUSA Retractable Leashes: www.flexiusa.com
Global Pet Finder: www.globalpetfinder.com
GoTags Personalized Collars: www.gotags.com
Gucci Heart and Bone Dog Pendant: www.gucci.com
Harness Play Pack: www.petsatplay.com
Hear Now Collar: www.thehearnow.com

Hug-A-Dog Harness: www.hug-a-dog.com
Les Poochs Collars and Leashes: www.lespoochs.com
Life Is Good Collars and Leashes: www.lifeisgood.com
The Pet's Jeweler Diamond and Gold Dog Tags: www.thepetsjeweler.com
Pick of the Glitter Swarovski Crystal Collars: www.petglitter.com
Posh Pooch: www.posh-pooch.com
Rouge New York: www.rougenewyork.com
Sally Harrell Dog Tags: www.sallyharrell.net
A Tail We Could Wag Collars and Leashes: www.tailwags.com
Tiffany Dog Tags: www.tiffany.com
WackyWalk'r: www.wackywalkr.com

Beds

Crypton Dog Bed: www.cryptonfabric.com
Fatboy Doggie Lounge: www.fatboyusa.com
Gel-Pedic Pet Bed: www.gelpedic.com
Louisdog Blue House: www.louisdog.com
Lucky Dog Furcedes Sports Car Bed: www.shopluckydog.com
Petsafe Wellness Bed: www.petsafe.net
Pet Tent: www.pettents.com
Pluscious Pet Décor: www.pluscious.com
Sleep-N-Store Bed: www.petsatplay.com
Snooty Pets Sleigh Bed: www.snootypets.com
Wouf Poof Leather Bone Bed: www.woufpoof.com

Carriers and Crates

Gucci: www.gucci.com
Hug-A-Dog Seatbelt Harness and Doggy Catcher: www.hug-a-dog.com
Jacques Traugott Pet Carriers: www.aurorapetproducts.com
Louisbag and Sports Bag Grand: www.louisdog.com
Sherpa Bag Deluxe, Sherpa-on-Wheels, and Pet Totes: www.sherpapet.net
Pet Lookout Car Booster Seat: www.kyjen.com
Petmate: www.petmate.com
Pet Stow-Away: www.globalpetproducts.com

Posh Pooch Carriers: www.posh-pooch.com
PuppyPurse: www.puppypurse.com
SkyKennel: www.petedge.com

Toys and Activities

GoDogGo Ball Launcher: www.buygodoggo.com
Leo: www.caninegenius.com
Life Is Good Flying Disc: www.lifeisgood.com
Louisdog: www.louisdog.com

Accessories for Pets and People

Exposures Custom Photo Collage Canvas, Note Cards, and Notecube: www.exposuresonline.com
Nintendogs: www.nintendo.com
PawPrints Jewelry: www.pawprintsjewelry.com
PhotoStamps.com: www.photostamps.com
Unique Products Photo Checks: www.uniquechecks.com

Travel Products and Services

Doggles Dog Eyewear: www.doggles.com
Home-N-Go Pet Pen: www.petedge.com
Outward Hound Pet-Saver Lifejacket: www.kyjen.com
Pet Friendly Travel: www.petfriendlytravel.com
Pets on the Go: www.petsonthego.com
Puppy Travel: www.puppytravel.com
Take Your Pet: www.takeyourpet.com

Index

continued

Photo Credits

Howell™ Gift Collection

More Great Books for Dog Lovers

Want to cook up homemade dog treats using canine-tested, veterinarian-approved recipes, teach your dog how to behave in polite society, get the scoop on caring for pint-size dogs, or celebrate your bond with your best friend? These fun books give you lots of information and make terrific gifts for your pet-loving friends.

Available at howellbookhouse.com and wherever books are sold.

Howell Book House™
An Imprint of **WILEY**
Now you know.